The Patriots of Nantucket

OSCAR MANDEL

The Patriots of Nantucket
A romantic comedy
of the American Revolution

A SPECTRUM PRODUCTIONS BOOK

LOS ANGELES, CALIFORNIA

Manufactured in the United States of America by **Gutenberg 2000**.

Library of Congress Catalog Card Number: 75-37367
ISBN 0-914502-02-6

Foreword

The Patriots of Nantucket began as a transplant to American soil of *Les Espagnols en Danemarck*, a delightful little play which Prosper Mérimée published in 1825 under the name of Clara Gazul. My own comedy quickly took on a character and purpose of its own (not to mention its bulk), which led it far from its source; and yet even now a few lines are absolute translations from Mérimée's text.

I wrote a first version in 1971, made a thoroughgoing revision in 1973, and have tampered with the text practically to the printer's doorstep.

In conveying the action from Denmark to Nantucket, I have taken a number of minor liberties with history. Thus, there was no British detachment posted on the island of Nantucket, no privateering commissions were granted as early as June 1775, and I am sure that no female French agent visited Sherburne (as the town was called at the time) in 1775 or in any other year. Other liberties are of the same feathery weight and consequence.

Many of the names I have used belong to Nantucket families still living on the island today. I have distributed these names quite arbitrarily and no allusion to any historical person or family is intended.

O.M.

Characters

Colonel Elias Starbuck, *54 years old.*

Nicholas Starbuck, *his nephew, 33.*

Thomas Weamish, *loyalist Judge of the Peace, 36.*

Henry Wallis, *confidential agent to the Starbucks, in his forties.*

Captain Alexander Cuff, *in command of a British detachment of marines, about 50.*

Enoch Swain, *proprietor of a tavern.*

Joshua Mamack, *an Indian man of all trades.*

Obed Coffin, *a seaman.*

Voice of Mr. Applegate, *a refugee from Concord.*

The Marquise de Tourville, *46 years old.*

Madeleine, *her daughter, 20.*

Jenny, *maid to the Weamish family.*

Ruth, *maid to the Starbuck family.*

The action takes place in and around Sherburne, Nantucket, from Tuesday, June 20 to Saturday, June 24, 1775.

SCENE ONE

(*Tuesday, June 20, 1775. Late morning. The two-story residence of JUDGE THOMAS WEAMISH in Sherburne, Nantucket. We are in the cheerful second-story sitting room. The only blemish in the room is that one windowpane is broken. JUDGE WEAMISH, a portly gentleman, is sitting at an elegant writing-table and concluding a letter to his mother*)

WEAMISH. "For the rest, my dear mamma, the weather today is but middling fair and somewhat blustery, as if the (*he hesitates*) united? — conjoined? (*He writes*) conjoined elements deplored the absence of one whom not a few among the natives of the island call the queen-mother of Nantucket. Speed, speed to these shores again, for our human storms require a hand such as yours that knoweth how to chide the weak and chastise the guilty. Ever your devoted son, Thomas. Mailed at Sherburne, Nantucket, Tuesday, the 20th of June, 1775." (*He dries the letter and rings a bell*)

(*Enter JENNY*)

JENNY. Yes, Mr. Weamish?

WEAMISH. When the post boy comes, tell him I have a letter for him.

JENNY. I will, Mr. Weamish. I saw Josh Mamack coming up the street, sir.

WEAMISH. It's about time! Catch him and send him up at once.

JENNY. Yes, sir.

(*She leaves. WEAMISH re-reads his letter with great enjoyment*)

WEAMISH. "Dearest mamma. God grant that this letter find you in the full enjoyment of your customary health and cheerful spirits. Need I tell you how sorely you are missed by all your friends in town? To fly to an ailing sister, a despondent and helpless brother-in-law, in the midst of an embattled Boston, within hearing of cannon fire, insulted daily by a rabble of treacherous (*he pauses, then inserts*) 'and unprincipled' villains, who, like froward children, dare to question the mild authority of a monarch beloved of all his rational subjects; to rush, I say, to a sister and brother (*he makes another insert*) 'cruelly expelled from their ancestral home at Cambridge'; to nurse them in their affliction; to comfort them for the loss of property, familiar grounds and acquaintances; all this proves you a Saltonstall, the proud daughter of a governor, and sister-in-law to a royal Councillor of Massachusetts. But let me descend from these heights, and commend myself to Dr. Brattle and to your dear sister, my aunt. Pray tell them they acted wisely in taking shelter in Boston under the victorious wings of his Excellency our governor and general, who, if reports tell true, hath recently beaten the impudent rebels out of Charlestown, and will now drum them handily out of the entire province. Alas, how I wish that I myself could wield a sword in these stirring times, rise to defend my king, and scourge the contumacious mob! But the robe enjoins its own duties, the law hath its own heroes. My sphere, at the moment, is our dear county of Nantucket, and here I mean to sustain his Majesty's mild rule and enforce his just decrees. What if you and I, my dear mamma, permit ourselves, in the intimacy of our household, to nurse the virtuous hope that Governor Gage will see fit some day soon to call me to his side, perhaps into his Council, to serve my king in a wider and nobler field of activity? I make no secret of my feelings. I do not care if a hint should come to the governor's ear that Thomas Weamish, who suffered for his king in the time of the Stamp Act, and who now once again beholds his windows shattered as the reward of his loyalty, that this same Thomas Weamish burns with a noble ambition to sacrifice his repose on the altar of our cherished colony. But you, my dear mamma, will know better than anyone how to convey these not unworthy sentiments to General Gage. Speak to him apart at the next assembly, when music hath made him cheerful. For is it fitting that a son of yours should pine away in a rude colonial outpost, among uncouth fishermen and Quakers, distant from elegant society—"

(*Enter JENNY and JOSHUA MAMACK, carrying tools*)

JENNY. Here's Josh, Mr. Weamish; and here is a letter for you.

MAMACK. Good day to you, sir.

WEAMISH (*taking the letter*). Well well, Mr. Mamack; very good of you to call on us, I'm sure. (*MAMACK scratches his head*) I'll attend to you in a moment. Is the post boy downstairs, Jenny?

JENNY. Yes, Mr. Weamish. The mail packet will be sailing a bit early this afternoon on account of the weather.

WEAMISH (*seals the letter to his mother*). Give him this, and pay him, will you?

JENNY. Yes, sir.

(*She leaves*)

WEAMISH (*showing the broken windowpane*). Here, Mr. Mamack.

MAMACK. Yah. I seed it. Same one they break nine years ago. Mamack good memory. Trouble trouble.

WEAMISH. Why, Mr. Mamack, has it taken you four days to find your way here?

MAMACK (*puzzled*). Find my way here?

WEAMISH. To answer my summons, Mamack. Am I to sit in this room for an entire week while the wind whistles through a broken window?

MAMACK. I mean to come right away quickly, Judge—

WEAMISH. But—?

MAMACK. Well—

WEAMISH. Well well well! Well what?

MAMACK. Well—I got a large family to support, I got a position in the community—

WEAMISH. A position in the—! A carpenter—a glazer—a jack Indian with a position in the community! So this is the new spirit blowing over the land! And what has your precious position in the community to do with my broken window, Mr. Mamack?

MAMACK. Aw, I was only talking, Judge. I fix that window fast.

WEAMISH. I insist that you tell me!

MAMACK. Well—

WEAMISH. Well?

MAMACK. Well, the folks around here see you comfy cozy with Captain Cuff and Mr. Applegate—

WEAMISH. Aha.

MAMACK. There's a heap of bad feeling on the island, Judge, like a wind, speak East, speak West, a cold wicked wind. But I don't meddle none in white man's business. I don't sit down into no committees.

WEAMISH. Committees, eh? I assure you I know all about their rebel committees.

MAMACK (*grinning*). They know all about you that you know all about them. They say you and Mr. Applegate hush hush at night, in the dark, only one candle, you write names with ink in a book.

WEAMISH. Rubbish!

MAMACK. But maybe they write names too, eh?

WEAMISH. Vicious agitators!

MAMACK. I better fix that window. Big storm stepping out of sky.

WEAMISH. And so these patriotic gentlemen have tried to keep you from mending my window.

MAMACK. They call a small meeting about it.

WEAMISH. A meeting! A meeting about my window!

MAMACK. Small meeting, Judge. A bowl of cider and a pipe in Swain's tap room. I said to them, I said, "Gentlemen, who am I? Josh Mamack, Pokanoket tribe, honest worker, no rum hardly ever, I must mend the Judge's window, not decent to keep the Judge in draft." And they said, "Go, friend, go in peace."

WEAMISH. So now it's the rebel committee that runs Nantucket! The magistrates and the selectmen no longer count. Tell me, Mr. Mamack, while you gentlemen were guzzling cider and puffing on your pipes, was not the vandal's name mentioned by chance?

MAMACK. Who?

WEAMISH. The window breaker's name!

MAMACK. The window breaker? O Lord—I don't know—
WEAMISH. Mr. Mamack, I am the chief magistrate of this county.
MAMACK. I know, sir. We're awful proud of you.
WEAMISH. I order you to speak. Who broke that window? One of the
Coffins? Young Macy? Coleman? Hussey's children?
MAMACK. How would I know? How would anybody know? But I have an
idea, Judge.
WEAMISH. Aha!
MAMACK. Because it's the same window what break when you was stamp
distributor—
WEAMISH. What of it?
MAMACK. I better fix that pane. I talk too much.
WEAMISH. Don't go near that window! Finish what you were about to say!
MAMACK. Yes, sir. I figure the moment I come in, I says to myself, by cod,
Mamack, it must be the same spirit which done it in sixty-six. Spirit, he
smashed like he was trying to tell you, "Watch out, Judge Weamish, the
people don't have forgotten!"
WEAMISH (*tremulous*). Spirit be damned! Rogues and rascals! They will not
forgive a man for carrying out British law. Thank God for Captain Cuff!
Fifty redcoats should suffice to curb these Sons of Liberty.
MAMACK. Oh, they don't like the redcoats, Judge Weamish. They don't like
the redcoats none whatsomever.
WEAMISH. I wonder why not!
MAMACK. We don't see so many soldiers since the French War. (*Casually*)
How long they going to stay, Judge?
WEAMISH. Forever, damn it! Go mend that window!
MAMACK. Yes, Judge.
(*He begins to work. WEAMISH paces up and down in some agitation*)
WEAMISH (*to himself*). Impudent heathens!
(*Drums and fifes are heard outside*)
MAMACK. Here come the soldiers now.
(*WEAMISH goes to another window, opens it, and waves*)
WEAMISH. Proud looking lads!
MAMACK. Good boys. Good for Nantucket, I say to everybody. Keep the
peace. Mind, I don't meddle, white folks know best.
(*The detachment is drilling below*)
MAMACK. Listen to them! Rat tat tat!
WEAMISH. Sturdy lads! One, two, one, two, shoulder arms!
MAMACK. What's your opinion, Judge? They going to hold down the
harbor? Put a few fellows in jail? Take our ships away from us?
WEAMISH (*smug*). We'll see. Captain Cuff has orders from General Gage to
make no move without my consent.
MAMACK (*whistling*). One day, spirit tell me and tell me sure, one day you
going to be Royal Duke in London. Mark Mamack's words, your mummy,
she be the proudest lady from here to Boston.
WEAMISH (*inspecting Mamack's work*). Good work, Mr. Mamack.

MAMACK. Thank you, sir, it's close to finished.
(*The detachment is moving off. Weamish waves again*)
WEAMISH. Ah, there's Colonel Starbuck. Colonel Starbuck!
VOICE OF STARBUCK. Good morning, Judge!
WEAMISH. Were you watching the drill all this time?
VOICE. Indeed I was!
WEAMISH. I defer to your military experience, Colonel. But to my civilian eyes these lads performed like a sturdy and reliable lot.
VOICE. A splendid set of young men, Judge Weamish; England's best, I'm sure.
WEAMISH (*without guile*). What a comfort to have them in our midst, is it not?
VOICE. It certainly is. Well, Judge, I'm on my way to the wharves. We're unloading a consignment of seasoned timber. It may be our last for many a day.
WEAMISH. I won't detain you, Colonel. Isn't that Mr. Applegate approaching?
VOICE. I believe it is. Good day to you, Judge.
WEAMISH. Good day, Colonel. Commend me to your sparkish nephew. Greetings, Mr. Applegate!
VOICE OF MR. APPLEGATE. Good morning, Judge! Nippy day for June, isn't it?
WEAMISH. Ah, you don't know our Nantucket as yet, Mr. Applegate. At Concord you were snugly sheltered in your trees, if I may say so. Here the wind blows, the clouds scour the land . . .
VOICE. Still, better the anger of the elements than the fury of disloyal men.
WEAMISH. True and affecting words, Mr. Applegate. A pity you missed the bracing spectacle just now. One of Captain Cuff's sergeants parading his men. Such a comforting sight.
VOICE. Good boys! There'll be brisk work for them on this island presently, if my presentiment don't lie.
WEAMISH. I shall tell Jenny to open the door.
VOICE. No, thank you kindly. I am dining an hour from now with Captain Cuff. Besides, I've no wish to intrude upon your elegant visitors.
WEAMISH. What elegant visitors, Mr. Applegate? This is Joshua Mamack, a plain laborer.
MAMACK. At your service, Mr. Applegate.
VOICE. I'm astonished! The two ladies who debarked from the New York packet—
WEAMISH. When? Who? I know nothing about the matter! Two ladies?
VOICE. Well then, I am the bringer of good tidings, or so I hope. Two foreign ladies. They came ashore this morning, drove to Swain's, and will undoubtedly be calling on you before noon. So I was told by the ship's master, Captain Frobish by name.
WEAMISH. I'm speechless! Allow me to take my leave of you, Mr. Applegate—I must prepare—two foreign ladies—oh dear, oh dear—

VOICE. I'll stop by this evening for news.

WEAMISH. Jenny! Jenny!

MAMACK. Sounds like a treat. Two ladies. Too bad Mrs. Weamish had to be in Boston.

(*JENNY appears*)

WEAMISH. Jenny, two guests will be arriving any moment!

JENNY. What are you talking about, Mr. Weamish?

WEAMISH. Two foreign ladies are coming! Don't stare at me, for goodness' sake! Mr. Applegate told me the news through the window. Hurry, tidy the house—perhaps they speak no English.

JENNY. The house is always tidy, Mr. Weamish.

WEAMISH. Dust the vestibule again. And prepare a collation. Use the silver. Hurry, while I brush—

(*The doorbell rings*)

JENNY. Too late.

WEAMISH. They must have rounded the street corner! Dear me—I'm totally unfit—but I'll have to make do. Go, Jenny, and let me not hear any milkpail familiarities—

JENNY (*peeved*). I'll do my best, Mr. Weamish.

(*She leaves*)

WEAMISH. Mamack—

MAMACK. Just a bit more putty, your honor.

WEAMISH. All right, but leave quietly. I shall settle with you another time.

MAMACK. Oh, don't you worry 'bout settling.

WEAMISH. Try not to bang anything.'

(*WEAMISH attempts to preen himself under MAMACK's stare. Enter JENNY, too overwhelmed to say much of anything, MADAME DE TOURVILLE, and MADELEINE. Both ladies speak impeccable English, but MADAME DE TOURVILLE has kept a slight French accent*)

JENNY. This is—

AIMEE. I am Aimée de Tourville. This is my daughter Madeleine. Am I addressing Judge Thomas Weamish?

WEAMISH. You are. Allow me to welcome you—and forgive my unpresentable—Jenny! Chairs! Such an unexpected honor—

AIMEE. In what sense unexpected, Mr. Weamish? Did I not pronounce my name clearly?

WEAMISH. Beautifully—pray sit—(*to Madeleine*) I beg you—Jenny, you know what to do.

JENNY. Yes, sir.

(*She hastily withdraws. MAMACK is gawking*)

AIMEE. I see an unopened letter on your escritoire, Judge Weamish. Its contents might have relieved you of your astonishment.

WEAMISH. Letter? (*He flings himself on the letter Jenny had given him before*) The press of business—night and day—may I?

AIMEE. You may and you must.

WEAMISH (*opens the letter*). Governor Gage! (*He sinks into his chair; then, recollecting who the writer is, leaps up again)* "My dear Weamish—"

AIMEE. Who is this man?

WEAMISH. Who—? Oh—nobody, madam, a common laborer mending my—Mamack, come back this afternoon.

MAMACK. Yes, your honor.

(He puts on his cap, bows and leaves)

AIMEE. The colonies are at war, Judge Weamish. A poodle could be a spy.

WEAMISH. I assure you—every measure has been taken—

AIMEE. Pray read the letter. Don't fidget, Madeleine.

WEAMISH. "My dear Weamish, Do not under any circumstances allow any man of rank to leave your island until further advice reaches you."

(AIMEE has stood up and walks casually about the room. She suddenly flings open the door, revealing the stupefied figure of Josh MAMACK. WEAMISH stops reading. Everybody stares at everybody. MAMACK doffs his cap)

WEAMISH *(thundering)*. What were you doing behind that door?

MAMACK. I forgot my chisel.

(AIMEE walks to the window, picks up the chisel between two fingers, and hands it over to MAMACK)

MAMACK. Thank you, ma'am.

(He vanishes and AIMEE closes the door)

AIMEE. War, Judge Weamish, war.

WEAMISH. To be sure, but—this was the same—an untutored Indian—

AIMEE. Pray continue your letter.

WEAMISH. Ah yes. Let me see. "Similar instructions have been sent to Captain Cuff. On the same day as you receive this, or shortly thereafter, the Marquise de Tourville—" *(he gapes)*

AIMEE. Come, my dear Judge, we are two-legged animals all the same. Read on.

WEAMISH. "The Marquise de Tourville—*(he bows to AIMEE)* accompanied by her daughter—*(he bows to MADELEINE)* will arrive at Sherburne with verbal orders that you are to obey implicitly. Madame de Tourville— *(he bows to AIMEE)* is well known to me and to their Excellencies the Governor and Lieutenant-Governor of New York. She will name the gentlemen who are the objects of our present concern, and inform you of the high importance we attach to her mission."

(Enter JENNY)

JENNY. Chocolate and buttered buns.

WEAMISH. Get out! Not now!

AIMEE. Tut tut. Why not now? Madeleine, you haven't said a word all morning. Are you for a little refreshment?

MADELEINE. I should love a cup of chocolate.

WEAMISH. Delightful! *(To JENNY)* Why are you standing there like a statue? Serve the ladies. Ah, Marquise, your visit gives me unspeakable pleasure. Nantucket will never be the same—I hope! *(To MADELEINE)* Did you enjoy a fair crossing from New York?

MADELEINE. Very—

AIMEE (*loud*). Not fair at all. The weather proved unseasonably rough, and for Madeleine's sake we decided to rest a few days before resuming our journey to Canada. (*To JENNY*) That will do, my girl.

(*WEAMISH grimaces at Jenny, who leaves in a daze*)

AIMEE. This is the story we shall allow to be spread, my dear Judge. Delicious chocolate.

WEAMISH. You are too kind.

AIMEE. It is no lie, however, that we are proceeding north. Now that the rebels have taken Fort Ticonderoga, I am informed that they will attempt to secure Canada.

WEAMISH. Secure Canada! Ha! That's a bone on which the dogs will choke at last.

AIMEE. Your confidence is heartening. But General Carleton, who commands in Canada, is far from easy in his mind. I am going there to animate our French people against the rebels. That, however, is neither here nor there. My daughter and I have been sent to Sherburne to investigate Colonel Elias Starbuck and his nephew Nicholas. You look surprised, Judge Weamish.

WEAMISH. Surprised? Not I!

AIMEE. Can it be that you entertain no suspicions in that quarter?

WEAMISH. I do entertain suspicions. Yes! I suspect everybody! This island is a hatchery of rebels!

AIMEE. That is more than I can say. My instructions are limited to the two Starbucks. Are they presently on the island?

WEAMISH. Of course. I would never—I spoke with Colonel Starbuck a few minutes ago. From this window. Ha! He was watching a British sergeant drilling his men. Tell me, Marquise, what are they guilty of? I'll proceed with every severity known to the law.

AIMEE. Who said they were guilty of anything? I spoke of suspicions. You know of course that Colonel Starbuck fought side by side with Colonel Washington in fifty-nine.

WEAMISH. Colonel Washington?

AIMEE. And with General Amherst at Montreal in 1760.

WEAMISH. With General Amherst was it? Hm. Allow me to advise you, Marquise, that Colonel Starbuck has a brother serving at this very moment in the congress of traitors at Philadelphia.

AIMEE. A cousin, I believe.

WEAMISH. Though he himself laughs at the matter, babbles about his loyal relations in Boston, and tells the world he has been a peaceful merchant for fourteen years.

AIMEE. Perhaps he is. In the meantime, it appears that Colonel Washington is to be appointed by the rebels to a particularly brilliant post of command. This cannot have reached you as yet.

WEAMISH. I assure you, Marquise, that we receive prompt and accurate intelligence here.

AIMEE. Then you know that the rebels who now besiege Boston are anxious to enlist capable officers to lead their miserable bands.

WEAMISH. They'll never find them.

AIMEE. Perhaps you will put two and two together. Or, if inconvenient, one and one.

WEAMISH. Of course. A terrifying plot—

AIMEE. What terrifying plot?

WEAMISH (to MADELEINE). May I pour again? Ah, such a winning smile. You were saying, Marquise?

AIMEE (with a sigh). We believe—that is to say, Governor Gage believes— that Colonel Starbuck has been approached to play a considerable part in the siege of Boston.

WEAMISH. Precisely as I surmised. I'll have him arrested after my dinner.

AIMEE. You must be jesting, my dear Judge.

WEAMISH. Why?

AIMEE. One doesn't arrest a valuable man upon a suspicion and create a popular disturbance. Quite on the contrary, let us hope that the rumors are false and that His Majesty can count on the Starbucks. My mission here is to take accurate soundings and to instruct you accordingly. Fortunately, as Frenchwomen we are thought to be the Yankees' natural allies and Britain's natural enemies. I'll see to it that my calling on you is dismissed as a frigid courtesy.

WEAMISH. A clever game, Marquise.

AIMEE. Now. We have taken rooms at your only inn—whatever you call it.

MADELEINE. Swain's Tavern, mamma.

AIMEE. Thank you, dear. There we shall find occasion to chat with the natives, place a few questions, distribute a trifle of coins, and meet the Starbucks themselves. As the old one's a widower, and the young one a bachelor, both are sure to be found in a tap room. I expect to have all the facts within three days.

WEAMISH. This is a disappointment to me. (He looks at MADELEINE)

AIMEE. Why?

WEAMISH. You land on this poor island of ours—diffusing the radiance of Versailles—snatches of music—ridottos—rank and fashion—and now you dash all my hopes by telling me we must be enemies.

AIMEE. I have not been at Versailles since 1757, my dear Judge, the year my husband, may God have mercy on his soul, took his regiment to Canada.

WEAMISH. You followed him.

AIMEE. Of course. I am a Fapignac!

WEAMISH. Ah! (To MADELEINE) Poor child!

AIMEE. Madeleine was born in France. At the age of three she was fatherless in Canada.

WEAMISH. The horrors of war.

AIMEE. The Marquis was carried off by the smallpox.

WEAMISH. Bitter, bitter. What can I possibly do to comfort you during your stay? Needless to say, I offer you my house.

AIMEE. True American courtesy, Judge Weamish. But you have understood the reasons which compel us to endure your tavern.

WEAMISH. I shudder.

MADELEINE. It seems like a pretty place, with a view upon the ocean.

WEAMISH. Pretty enough for our islanders, I daresay. But, my dear ladies, you cannot conceive what it is for a man of breeding to live among fishermen, Quakers, Indians, farmers—with never a ball, a concert, or a play to relieve the tedium. I am—if I may take the liberty of mentioning it—the grandson of a governor.

AIMEE. Governor Saltonstall, is it not?

WEAMISH. Yes.

AIMEE. Your mother, Mrs. Weamish, is presently in Boston?

WEAMISH. To my sorrow, she is. Nursing her sister and her brother-in-law, both refugees from Cambridge, and sadly come down since their flight.

AIMEE. What is the news from Boston? We have been on board our wretched vessel since Saturday.

WEAMISH. Ah Marquise, why didn't you remind me before? I am in a position to give you news of capital importance.

AIMEE. Oh?

WEAMISH. A magnificent victory at Charlestown.

AIMEE (*happily*). Under Gage's command?

WEAMISH. Indirectly, madam. He dispatched General Howe across the bay to give chase to the villains who had occupied the hills overlooking Boston. Their leader, a firebrand named Joseph Warren, was left dead on the field, and the Whiggish dogs were driven from the peninsula licking their desperate wounds.

MADELEINE. I pray they can still be reconciled. Your country is so beautiful—so plentiful—I feel that God has meant it for peace.

WEAMISH. They shall have peace shortly, mademoiselle. Our generals are making ready to sweep the province clear of rebels. They are a loose collection of shallow rascals, all brave enough behind their fences, but routed by the first volley of our muskets. They cannot enlist respectable officers—ah, you said so yourself, Marquise. This is June. We shall have peace before winter, I assure you.

AIMEE. In the meantime, you and Captain Cuff—

WEAMISH. Have you met the Captain, madam?

AIMEE. Not yet. But you and he will see that no personage of any significance leaves the island. This must be gone about discreetly, of course.

WEAMISH. I have heard of no one who has declared a wish to leave.

AIMEE. Good. Madeleine and I will repair to our inn—

WEAMISH. May I put my mother's calash at your disposal?

AIMEE. By no means. I have hired what appears to be the only chaise in Nantucket.

WEAMISH. I am mortified.

AIMEE. I had hoped for a phaeton, but this is not New York.

WEAMISH. Alas.

AIMEE. Still, I have worked under worse conditions. Madeleine!

(*JENNY rushes in*)

JENNY. Begging your pardon. (*She curtseys*) Mr. Weamish, there's Mr. Starbuck, the young one, storming downstairs and wanting to see you at once.

WEAMISH. What shall I do? Young Starbuck of all people! Here's another way out. You didn't tell him these ladies are here, did you?

JENNY. How else could I keep him from rushing upstairs?

AIMEE. The girl is right. Come now, show Mr. Starbuck upstairs. No harm at all.

JENNY. Yes, ma'am.

(*She hurries out*)

AIMEE. We'll turn this to our advantage. It's a piece of luck that we should meet one of the Starbucks so soon.

(*Enter NICHOLAS STARBUCK*)

NICHOLAS. Judge Weamish, where is our mail? I know you are entertaining distinguished visitors; pray accept my sincerest apologies. (*He bows to the LADIES*) I am Nicholas Starbuck, gentle ladies, my bad temper was given me by the gods, I was not consulted. Sir: myself and my uncle are expecting important commercial letters from the mainland. Three weeks have gone by without a single message. Today the New York packet arrives. (*Again to the LADIES*) And by the way, allow me to report that I happened to see your luggage safely delivered at Swain's Tavern. (*Back to WEAMISH*) Today, I repeat, the packet from New York puts in. Several sacks of mail emerge from the captain's cabin. Your constable George Hackbutt removes them. Now sir: I make no accusations, but I demand of you, as chief magistrate of this island, whether orders have been issued to seize, withhold, or destroy our mail.

WEAMISH. My dear Mr. Starbuck, calm yourself—

NICHOLAS. I am enraged, but in full control of myself.

WEAMISH (*to AIMEE*). May I introduce?

AIMEE. Of course.

WEAMISH. Mr. Starbuck, this is the Marquise de Tourville, and this is Mademoiselle de Tourville.

NICHOLAS. Honored.

AIMEE. Charmed. I sympathize with your anger, Mr. Starbuck.

WEAMISH. And so do I. Nothing is being withheld *here*, Mr. Starbuck. What is confiscated in New York, or intercepted on the way, I cannot tell. *My* orbit is limited to these few islands.

AIMEE. We were not intercepted, were we, Madeleine?

MADELEINE. No.

AIMEE. But why, Mr. Starbuck, should you in particular be harassed? Do the authorities have reasons—?

NICHOLAS. No reasons whatever. Thank you for your concern, Marquise; my remarks are addressed to the Judge.

AIMEE (*laughing*). Forgive a meddlesome old woman, Mr. Starbuck; I'm rather too accustomed to ordering people about. Friends? (*She reaches out her hand*)

NICHOLAS (*kissing it*). Friends.

WEAMISH. Come, sir, sit down with us. I predict that you shall have your letters before the week is over. Let me propose something a shade stronger than warm chocolate before we all dine together.

NICHOLAS. Judge Weamish, if I'm not mistaken, this is a product of contraband.

WEAMISH (*laughing*). Justice is blindfolded.

AIMEE. A little concession to the good life, eh?

WEAMISH. Ah, how else can a gentleman survive? Nothing but sperm oil, tar, pitch . . .

NICHOLAS. All the same, old Mr. Weamish made a pretty thing out of your detested sperm oil. (*To the LADIES*) Manufactured sperm candles. (*Mock aside*) A fortune!

WEAMISH. To be sure. We colonials must be content to derive from trade and industry.

AIMEE. Don't apologize, sir. I have lived on your continent long enough to value the spirit of commerce.

WEAMISH. This is true elevation of mind! Ah, how I feel the absence of my mother. She is worthy of your acquaintance, Marquise.

AIMEE. Let us drink to her prompt return, shall we?

NICHOLAS. With pleasure.

(*They all drink*)

WEAMISH. Thank you. And now, I propose a toast to His Excellency, Governor Gage. Will you join us, Mr. Starbuck?

NICHOLAS. With enthusiasm. To Tom Gage!

WEAMISH. And to his brilliant victory at Bunker Hill!

NICHOLAS. What brilliant victory?

WEAMISH. He doesn't know! Come, come, you're jesting.

NICHOLAS. No, I protest. No jest intended. What brilliant victory?

WEAMISH. At Charlestown, Mr. Starbuck, on Saturday, three days ago! Nonsense! You do know! Here's the account in the *Gazette and Post-Boy*.

NICHOLAS (*looking at the paper*). So that's the battle, is it? Upon my word, the engagement is so differently described in the *Spy* (*he pulls out a gazette of his own*) that I became confused.

WEAMISH. Rubbish! The *Spy*! A well-deserved name, I'll warrant.

AIMEE. You pique my curiosity, Mr. Starbuck. Tell us more. What *really* happened at the battle?

NICHOLAS. I seriously hope that this rebel sheet is lying, Marquise. I found it crumpled on the floor of the custom collector's office. It reports that over a thousand redcoats were killed and maimed.

MADELEINE. How dreadful!

WEAMISH. Stuff and nonsense! The rebels were driven from the peninsula!

NICHOLAS. The writer manfully confesses it: an admission which throws some flickers of likelihood upon the rest of his account. And if the rest be true, the British are broken at Boston.

WEAMISH. Pah! Your gazette cannot impose on a rational observer. Trust me, my kindhearted demoiselle. The rabble is not born that can slaughter the king's army in fair battle. However, this glee of yours, Mr. Starbuck, hardly accords with your recent vows of loyalty at the meeting house.

NICHOLAS. Glee? What glee? Long live King George, third of the name! My father left me a fine house in Boston, for which an officer of his Majesty's 47th, Major Sutcliffe, is paying me good rent. I am no rebel against my property!

AIMEE. I perceive that my daughter and I must keep our opinions to ourselves while residing in Sherburne. Before you came in, Mr. Starbuck, and before I knew, indeed, where the Judge's allegiance lay, I spoke rather too freely in favor of liberty.

WEAMISH. They being French, you see, and happy to see this division in our land. Not that I can hold a grudge against two pairs of beautiful eyes!

AIMEE. You are a charmer, sir. Who would have expected such elegant manners on this windy island?

WEAMISH. You will all remain for dinner, I hope. I shall give Jenny orders at once.

NICHOLAS. Not I, thank you. I've accounts to settle with Hugh Catchcart— that's my cooper, Marquise, if I may use the low word.

AIMEE. And we had better unpack and dine quietly in our rooms today. Another time, Judge.

(Enter JENNY)

JENNY. Excuse me, but it's Colonel Starbuck downstairs, who doesn't want to intrude but who'd like a word with you, Mr. Weamish.

NICHOLAS (to the ladies). My uncle.

WEAMISH. Ask him up.

(Exit JENNY)

WEAMISH (significantly). This is fortunate, Marquise. Colonel Starbuck is one of our leading citizens. (With his arm around NICHOLAS) The Starbucks are among the founders of Sherburne.

(Enter COLONEL STARBUCK)

WEAMISH. Come in, sir. Your nephew is here.

STARBUCK. I apologize. Egad, I see you are evenly paired without me. Well met, Nicholas.

WEAMISH. May I introduce, Marquise, Mademoiselle, this is Colonel Elias Starbuck; Colonel Starbuck, I have the honor to present you to the Marquise de Tourville and her fair daughter.

AIMEE. My Madeleine.

STARBUCK. Welcome to Nantucket, Marquise, Mademoiselle. I hope you will spend the summer with us.

AIMEE. Oh no, Colonel. We are traveling to my property near Montreal. But Madeleine found the crossing from New York excessively fatiguing. She's a delicate child, unlike her mother, who's as sturdy as a jailer's wife. I decided to break the journey, and to wait here for the next packet.

STARBUCK. That will give us the pleasure of keeping you for a whole week.

WEAMISH. You wanted a word with me, Colonel?

STARBUCK. In my capacity of selectman, my dear Judge. Tom Arthur happened, for some reason I know nothing of, to be rummaging in the attic of Timothy Morton's store. There he discovered a stock of tea hidden under several bushels of flour. He ran down with it in a rage and threw it all into the pond nearby. Morton raised a clamor; one of Captain Cuff's men came running, knocked Arthur to the ground, and dragged him off to jail.

WEAMISH. Heavenly mercies! My dear ladies—this is a grave incident—

AIMEE. Attend to it, sir, attend to it at once.

NICHOLAS. Since when is Captain Cuff the constable here? This must be stopped immediately.

STARBUCK. The question of jurisdiction is critical. I am deeply concerned.

WEAMISH. And I am all a-quiver. The rebels are showing their claws. To dump private property in a pond! Colonel, I beg you to step into my cabinet for a signed deposition.

STARBUCK. Gladly.

WEAMISH (to the LADIES) I humbly beg your permission—

AIMEE. Proceed, proceed.

(The two men leave)

MADELEINE. How dreadful—on such a tranquil island—here at least one might have hoped—

NICHOLAS. I must disillusion you, sweet lady; we are the same beasts here as they are in New York or London.

AIMEE. But why so much excitement over a sack of tea?

MADELEINE. You've forgotten, mother.

AIMEE. What have I forgotten? I'm an alien, I know so little about your politics—Nicholas. May I call you Nicholas?

NICHOLAS. No—unless you allow me to call your daughter—Madeleine.

AIMEE. Shall we petition her directly? Well, my child?

MADELEINE (shyly). You may.

NICHOLAS. This is a high privilege.

AIMEE. Now, Nicholas, tell me about this wearisome tea.

NICHOLAS. A symbol, Marquise, nothing more. Our brothers in Britain granted themselves a monopoly of the tea trade in the colonies—

AIMEE. Ah, now I remember.

NICHOLAS. And the colonies object.

AIMEE. You men! If you cannot make war over the gold mines of Peru, you will do it over a tea leaf.

NICHOLAS. Tea leaf is unjust, Marquise. Our Whigs speak of Liberty.

AIMEE. Are you a Whig, Mr. Starbuck?

NICHOLAS. Like yourself, Marquise, I forget. I attend to my business affairs.

AIMEE. You disappoint me. Or rather, I hope you are using discretion in front of two strangers. I confess my heart pounds to the drums of liberty. But I pray you do not mention this to Judge Weamish, who, between you and me, appears to be an ultra on the Tory side.

NICHOLAS. I promise to say nothing.

AIMEE. Were I a man, I would swim away from this island if need be and make for the hottest sector of the battlefield!

NICHOLAS. You too, Madeleine?

MADELEINE. For the sake of liberty—anything!

AIMEE (embracing MADELEINE). My daughter!

NICHOLAS. If the Judge should hear you!

AIMEE. This reminds me; now that we have done our duty to your magistrate—Madeleine, let's be on our way. Mr. Starbuck, may we expect you for tea—I should say coffee—or cider—I shall let you choose—but do call on us—your uncle and yourself—at Swain's Tavern at four.

NICHOLAS. At four? I believe I can answer for my uncle. We'll be most happy. Today's a blustery day—(WEAMISH and STARBUCK reenter) but on the next clear evening I engage to show you a sunset from the eastern part of this island that you will never forget.

WEAMISH. Our famous dusk at Sconset.

AIMEE. I look forward to it. Judge Weamish, you have entertained two helpless female travelers beyond their deserts. We shall ask for our revanche before long.

WEAMISH. Use me as you will, Marquise. But allow me to escort you to your chaise.

AIMEE. You are too kind.

STARBUCK. We follow in a moment.

AIMEE. Colonel, Mr. Starbuck.

(The two bow, and the LADIES, followed by WEAMISH, leave)

STARBUCK (hurriedly and in a whisper). A word with you, young Nick.

NICHOLAS. Yes?

STARBUCK. A message from the first mate of the New York packet: the Enterprise is anchoring off the Bluffs this afternoon or tonight.

NICHOLAS (excited). Wallis is landing in person! And here I came storming after the mail.

STARBUCK. Be careful, don't do any storming, do you hear? Wallis will bring important letters for both of us.

NICHOLAS. Uncle! They want you in command before Boston.

STARBUCK. Hush. I'll be a common private if necessary.

NICHOLAS. You don't fear that the Enterprise will make for the harbor, do you?

STARBUCK. Not if they see our signals. I have dispatched Mamack to Trot's Hills with instructions.

NICHOLAS. Good. Listen—quickly. This will help, by Jove! The French ladies have asked us for a collation at the tavern at four o'clock.

STARBUCK. Splendid. It's the best lookout we could hope for. Come along. We've tarried too long.

WEAMISH (outside). Colonel! Mr. Starbuck!

NICHOLAS. We're coming! I struck my knee against your confounded table, Judge, and have been rubbing the wound till I can walk again!

WEAMISH (same). So sorry!

NICHOLAS (*to his uncle*). Come along!
STARBUCK (*grinning*). Young devil!
(*They leave, NICHOLAS affecting a hobble*)

SCENE TWO

*(Tuesday, June 20. Late afternoon. The tap room of Swain's Tavern.
CAPTAIN CUFF is drinking grog. ENOCH SWAIN is behind the counter.)*

CUFF. Take another peek into the parlor, Mr. Swain, will you?

SWAIN. I'd rather not, Captain. The parlor door is closed, and I don't like—

CUFF. Hell's fires! You're a dainty fellow, Mr. Swain. Come, fill my bowl
again. I'll moisten my melancholy while our two Starbucks nibble cakes
with their French mistresses.

SWAIN. Captain!

CUFF. Do I hear cups clinking?

SWAIN. Very likely, Captain.

CUFF *(contemptuously)*. French gentlefolk!

SWAIN. Are they not to your liking, Captain?

CUFF. Why—look you, Mr. Swain—I exchanged twenty words with them
today—and when 'twas over, what with putting a ribbon upon every word
I spoke, I felt as weary as if I'd hauled a cannon up a mountainside. This
flimsy-whimsy is not for me. I'm a Yorkshire man, God strike me.

SWAIN. Well—I'm almost with you, Captain, on this particular point. The
devil's in all that luxury, for sure. You should have seen the uncommon
quantity of luggage.

CUFF. I saw it this morning. Let them enjoy it. Though they may own a
hundred gowns a piece, they can't do anything with what's under them that
your tinker's wife can't do as well, or better.

SWAIN. Captain!

(CUFF looks out the window)

CUFF. Wretched weather. As if this scurvy island of yours wasn't bleak
enough in the sunshine. I shall drivel of nothing but herring, cod and
whaleblubber when they fetter me down in Bedlam. Stranded on Nantucket
with two-score men like a derelict sergeant. Islanders plotting treason. Not
three friendly words to be got in a week's time. The women as sour as milk
a year old. God's bleeding body! More rum, Mr. Swain.

SWAIN. I must ask you in all humility, Captain Cuff, not to swear in this house. We are Quakers—

CUFF (*simultaneously*). We are Quakers—I know it, God damn your pokey faces! Y'are too virtuous to grin while you ram your women, but y'are willing enough to plot against your God-given King!

SWAIN. Captain Cuff—we are simple folk, fearful of the law, trembling before divine wrath—ah, here they are at last—

(*The parlor door opens, and the STARBUCKS enter the tap room*)

CUFF. Well met, gentlemen, I've been waiting for you. Let me have a word with you before you go.

(*They shake hands*)

STARBUCK. Good afternoon, Captain Cuff.

NICHOLAS. Captain, how are you?

CUFF. Vile. Soaking my gloom in Mr. Swain's rum. And your ladies? Awash in coffee?

STARBUCK. The ladies are a delight. Nick, I believe you have reason to agree with me. If the rogue knew how to blush, I swear you might toast bread on his cheeks. Come now, is not Madeleine a pretty name?

NICHOLAS. Ma-de-leine, uncle, you must say it after the French manner. The name is pretty, but 'tis the least pretty thing its owner has to show.

CUFF. Now that's spoken like a villain in a penny romance! Drink a bowl with me, gentlemen.

STARBUCK. Gladly. Mr. Swain, my nephew and I desire something a bit stronger than our genteel refreshment in the parlor.

CUFF. At last a sensible word. Sit down, my buccaneers.

(*NICHOLAS has been looking anxiously out the window*)

NICHOLAS. It's beginning to rain. The wind is whipping it in.

STARBUCK. Well, we'll make ourselves comfortable here for a while. Let's sit nearer the window, Captain. The light's growing dim.

SWAIN. Would you like a candle, Colonel?

STARBUCK. Oh no, not yet.

(*During what follows, STARBUCK and NICHOLAS will be stealing looks out the window*)

CUFF. Colonel, you and young Nick must help a fellow officer. I know y'are kith and kin with the natives here, but then again y'ave travelled, y'ave fought for your King, y'ave killed your share of Frenchmen from the Carolines to Quebec. Now comes the time again to show whether there's blood or muck in your veins.

NICHOLAS. That's a mighty diplomatic speech, Captain Cuff.

CUFF. True by God's gut—I'm brushing your fur a bit, but I've heard about you, Nick, you were an ensign at Montreal afore you shaved, and you fought the savages near Niagara Falls when General Amherst was commanding. It's no lie; I can name you the officers of every regiment that's been raised since the French wars began in the year fifty-four.

NICHOLAS. That's all water long ago under the bridge. What's on your mind, Captain?

CUFF. You know what's on my mind, damn it! Mr. Swain, kindly look after my horse, now that the rain is falling.

SWAIN. Yes, sir.

(*He leaves*)

CUFF (*leaning forward confidentially*). Look you, friends: sure as my mother bore me, I know there's powder, flints and bullets stowed away in a dozen holes up and down the island. And they're not meant for shooting whales, says Captain Cuff.

NICHOLAS. Whoever gave you this information is a fool. Why should anyone be hiding ammunition? This island is defenceless. Three of your frigates could level every house upon it, and never a man living on the mainland would lift a finger to help us.

CUFF. You tell this to your whaling crews, young Nick—do—they need to hear it. Because all the same they're making cartridges, and there's many a cache under a windmill or a meeting-house that could tell a tale on my side. I'm not willing—yet!—to send my troops out digging and delving—forty men is too little, God blast it, and if tempers flare we'll finish as manure for your cornfields. But you two—you can do the work quietly for me. God's nails, are you loyal men or not?

NICHOLAS. Are we loyal men?

STARBUCK (*interrupts with a gesture*). You're in the right, Captain. Nick and I, why, we meddle so little, it startled us to hear that the situation is as grave as you say.

CUFF. I tell you it is.

STARBUCK. Leave the matter in our hands. We know where to ask a discreet question or two. If your reports are correct, trust me—

(*Voices outside*)

VOICES. Man overboard! Man overboard!

(*The MEN leap up and open the windows. SWAIN comes running in*)

VOICES. He's lost! Where is he now? He's gone for sure! There he is again! Etc. ad libitum.

STARBUCK (*in a whisper, seizing NICHOLAS' arm*). Wallis!

CUFF (*shouting out the window*). Don't stand there, you ninnies! Plunge in!

SWAIN (*moaning*). It's raining into the room! (*He shuts his window*)

(*AIMEE and MADELEINE rush into the room*)

AIMEE. A man is drowning!

VOICES. The breakers are too rough—we can't launch her!

MADELEINE (*piteously, to NICHOLAS*). Won't anyone save him?

CUFF. Cowards one and all!

NICHOLAS (*to STARBUCK*). Let's go!

(*The STARBUCKS rush out, followed by CUFF. SWAIN tries to shut the windows, dry his property, pick up fallen objects, etc.; but MADELEINE tears open a window again and the two women peer outside, where the shouting continues*)

MADELEINE. I saw him! Nicholas! I'm sure I saw his head!

SWAIN (*still sweeping up*). Oh madam, how many of these I've witnessed in my day!

AIMEE. What's the young man doing?

MADELEINE. Nicholas! He's diving into the water! Stop him! Stop him! He'll drown!

(*She wants to rush out, but AIMEE holds her back*)

AIMEE. Where are you going, silly girl? Mr. Swain, close the window—the wind is drenching us!

MADELEINE. He'll die! Nobody else dared! (*To SWAIN*) You! Open the window again! (*SWAIN obeys reluctantly*) Faster! What do you see?

VOICES. Where is he?

VOICE OF STARBUCK. Nicholas! He's to your left!

SWAIN. I can't see—it's a murderous squall.

(*Enter CAPTAIN CUFF*)

CUFF. God blast it! What an island! I'm soaked for nothing!

MADELEINE. Captain, is he safe? Is Mr. Starbuck safe?

CUFF. Who knows? I can't swim, at any rate. But I trust the young fellow. They say he's scalped a brace of Indians with his bare teeth!

MADELEINE. I'm crying.

CUFF. Let's have a fire in that chimney, Mr. Swain, and be quick about it.

(*AIMEE is making MADELEINE drink something*)

AIMEE. Be still, silly goose — a young man you've barely met. Besides —

VOICES. There they are! Hurrah! Heads up! *Etc. ad lib.*

SWAIN. You see! God is merciful.

AIMEE. There, I told you.

MADELEINE. Oh God, keep him alive!

CUFF (*still drying himself*). Spare your tears, young miss; your laddy's a proper dolphin.

AIMEE. He's not our laddy, Captain Cuff. My daughter happens to be tender-hearted; she makes no distinction between strangers and relations. There, there, Madelon, all's well. (*In a whisper*) Good work, young lady.

(*Enter the MEN, carrying HENRY WALLIS*)

STARBUCK (*to the outside*). Keep everybody away, Mamack! Tell them to go home! (*Inside*) Make room! Make room! Over there, on the sofa!

MADELEINE. Yes — it's the best place!

SWAIN. Put this tablecloth under him, if you please.

NICHOLAS. Hang your tablecloth, man! Gently, gently. His head on the cushion.

(*They lie WALLIS down*)

CUFF. Go fetch a doctor, Swain; don't dawdle!

AIMEE. And have a bed made ready for the poor man.

SWAIN. Here? In my place?

STARBUCK. Never mind the bed. Go call the doctor. On your way!

(*Exit SWAIN*)

STARBUCK. We live a hundred yards from here, Marquise; he'll be more comfortable with us. Don't press too close upon him, all of you.

AIMEE (*to NICHOLAS*). Besides, what are *you* doing here? Go stand by the fire. Young hero! I must embrace you, wet or dry! Ah, so much emotion!

(*She embraces him*)
And you, Madeleine? Are you indifferent to this splendid action?
(*MADELEINE looks at NICHOLAS*)
NICHOLAS. You've cried!
(*She flings herself into his arms*)
MADELEINE. That was beautiful! Selfless!
NICHOLAS. You'll be horribly wet, Madeleine. Away from me, though I hate to say the words. Let's attend to the poor man.
STARBUCK. He's breathing regularly. Patience.
AIMEE. What's this?
STARBUCK. Nothing. A pouch around his neck.
(*He gently lifts WALLIS' head to take it*)
AIMEE. Let me see.
STARBUCK. It's nothing; a woman's picture —
AIMEE. How exciting — may I see?
STARBUCK (*to NICHOLAS*). Keep it safe for him, Nick.
(*NICHOLAS casually snuggles the pouch away and creates a diversion*)
NICHOLAS. Look, he opened his left eye! Marquise, will you help me undo these buttons?
CUFF. You're wrong. He's still out.
AIMEE. Perhaps we should lift his feet to make him give up the water he must have swallowed.
CUFF. That would really finish him.
WALLIS (*coming to*). What happened? Am I safe?
(*Exclamations ad lib*)
STARBUCK. Among strangers but safe — *strangers* but safe — do you hear me?
WALLIS. Yes. I understand. Thanks be to God Almighty.
AIMEE. Who are you, my good man?
STARBUCK. Let's not question him now.
WALLIS. Steward on the — on the —
STARBUCK. It doesn't matter.
AIMEE. Steward?
WALLIS. I was rowing ashore — for a barrel of oil — and some candles . . . Where's my pouch?
NICHOLAS. In my pocket, my good fellow. The portrait survived. Happy now? Well, the man's alive and conscious. Ready, uncle?
MADELEINE. Why not carry him up to our rooms?
AIMEE. A good thought. Colonel, take your brave nephew home. Captain Cuff and I will carry the poor steward to my bed; he has travelled enough for one day; and bid one of your servants bring a suit of dry clothes for him. Don't forget, if you please, that your doctor will be coming *here* to examine him.
STARBUCK. Tell him to call at my house.
(*He and NICHOLAS start to take WALLIS up. AIMEE pushes him down*)
AIMEE. What do *you* think, Captain? Is not mine the better plan?

CUFF. I don't care. Take him away, Colonel; I think our host Mr. Swain will be grateful to you.

STARBUCK. Help me, Nick. Oops! Can you walk, my friend?

WALLIS. If I put my arm your shoulder.

NICHOLAS (to the LADIES). As soon as I've changed into something respectable — (he sneezes)

MADELEINE. There! There! I knew it! You will die of a congestion. Hurry home!

NICHOLAS. But may I hurry back?

MADELEINE. Why?

STARBUCK (impatient). Nicholas!

NICHOLAS. To give you news of our castaway.

MADELEINE. Yes, do.

STARBUCK. Come along, Nicholas.

NICHOLAS. Marquise; Captain.

CUFF (shaking his hand). Well done, Mr. Starbuck. I'll take up swimming myself, by God!

(Exeunt, CAPTAIN CUFF holding the door open for them)

CUFF. The rain has stopped at any rate.

AIMEE. I wish, Captain, that you had seconded my request to keep the steward here.

CUFF. Why, Marquise? He'll be better cared for by the Starbucks than here, for I doubt that the fellow brought enough gold to satisfy Mr. Swain. This Mr. Swain, I assure you —

AIMEE. Let it pass, Captain.

CUFF. My homages to you, dear ladies; you may command me, day or night.

AIMEE. Thank you, Captain Cuff.

(He bows and leaves. AIMEE is in deep thought)

AIMEE. A strange affair.

MADELEINE. Why strange?

AIMEE. Look at you! Dieu me damne! You've fallen in love with that American Leander.

MADELEINE (playfully). Why do you say that, mother? Didn't you order me to be friendly with the suspects?

AIMEE. Pooh! I've never yet seen you so keen to do your duty.

MADELEINE. Don't scold me, mamma! You must admire him too. How brave he was! For the sake of an absolute stranger — no one else so much as removed his coat — and he plunges in — swims like a Neptune —

AIMEE. Swims like a Neptune! A duck can swim as well. Now we're in love with a fellow because he swims.

MADELEINE. Have it your way.

AIMEE. As for being selfless —

MADELEINE. To be sure. This steward is a pasha in disguise who will leave all his millions to Nicholas.

AIMEE. He may leave him something more important. Steward be hanged! You must be blind, my girl! Thank goodness I'm an expert, I snap at details.

MADELEINE. What details?

AIMEE. You weren't struck by that sealskin pouch? How worried he was about it?

MADELEINE. It was lovely of him to think of his sweetheart the moment he came to.

AIMEE. The girl's determined to be an idiot! To think that I raised you on Plutarch and Tacitus! I don't suppose you noticed how anxious the Colonel was to keep that pouch out of my hands.

MADELEINE. You're right; I didn't notice.

AIMEE. And you didn't think it was odd that a common cook should be wearing a silk shirt, ruffled wrist bands, and gold buttons; mind you, got up like a man of condition when he was out rowing a dinghy to take on a barrel of whale oil. Silly details, of course.

MADELEINE. He was a steward.

AIMEE. If he was a steward, a seaman should have been rowing his boat.

MADELEINE. Another detail.

AIMEE. Details, my dear girl, make all the difference between a professional and a dilettante. Without details we'd still be selling keys in Montreal. I suppose you've forgotten that dreadful winter in 1760 when we nearly died of the cold.

MADELEINE. In Montreal? I was five years old!

AIMEE. *I* remember my life from the day I was weaned. Another tell-tale difference between us. I can only say it again: your father must have been that clod of a bailiff, I wish I could remember his name, the one with the heavy jowls and the slow aa ôô aa . . . I've noticed the same slowness in you.

MADELEINE (*sadly*). I'd rather hear about the winter in Montreal.

AIMEE. Why not? Now that I may be able to use you at last, why not take a lesson from your mother? A lesson about details, for instance. How a sharp eye raised me high in the world.

MADELEINE. I thought you didnt't like me to know too much about the past.

AIMEE. True. But when I see you not quick enough to step around a puddle, I wonder did I overdo your ignorance. I didn't escape out of that key shop, or make friends with Tom Gage, by singing ballads at the window. It never occurs to a child that his parents had to *arrive* where he found them when he was born.

(*She is sitting by the fire and poking it*)

MADELEINE. I'll try to learn from you, mother.

AIMEE. A cold, cold winter it was, the first under English rule. I was struggling to survive on that miserable shop. All my Number Two had left me was a dented sword and a tunic with braids, out of which, by the way, I made you the prettiest skirt. But food was scarce, and you were no Amazon, God knows; more than once I thought I'd lose you. Gage was a fair man, however, as Englishmen go. He gave an order, in French, to show you how fair he was, that beef was to sell at no more than ten sous the pound. I hadn't been in Montreal long enough to get special favors from the butchers. I'd run from one to the other, an ounce here, a slice there, sometimes as far as the Arsenal, knee-deep in snow or falling on the ice. Beef at ten sous, mutton twelve. You see what a memory I have. But somehow I was always dealt the worst cuts, meat that stank in spite of the cold, never a smidgeon more than my ration, and my pittance handed over the counter with sour distrustful faces. I was a newcomer, that's all. Pretty soon, though, I noticed a detail. Every butcher kept an almsbox prominently displayed for the hospital or the Ursulines. Nothing unusual about that, *you* would have said. Or rather, you wouldn't have noticed. I, instead, I was struck, the same as when I saw those frills on Mr. Steward. I thought, "How wonderfully generous we all are! Everybody's freezing and starving, but never a trip to the butcher's without a few pious coins into those boxes." And one day — another detail — I saw one of our good ladies of Montreal drop a coin and throw the butcher a wink. And that, my dear girl, is how I ceased to be Madame Pichot and became the Marquise de Tourville.

MADELEINE. You informed, mother?

AIMEE. I obeyed the law, my love; I am always on the sunny side of the law. If I hadn't married a jailwarden in Lyons on the sunny side of the law, I wouldn't have met the Vicomtesse de Brion in a cell —

MADELEINE. A vile poisoner; I wish you weren't always talking about her.

AIMEE. She was a brave woman; instead of crying over her brute of a husband, she poisoned him. When she came out to be hanged, my first husband cried like a baby and insisted on kissing her hand. I owe her everything I am. In the year we had her with us she taught me how to speak, dress and comport myself like a lady; accomplishments I've tried to pass on to an ungrateful daughter.

MADELEINE. I would have been glad to remain plain Mademoiselle Pichot, and run your key shop for you.

AIMEE. You have a low mind. I, instead, wrote to Monsieur Maturin, who was Gage's secretary, named myself, poor widow of Gustave Pichot, late sergeant in the light infantry, the butcher got twenty lashes, the almsboxes disappeared, and I quietly entered the Governor's service.

MADELEINE. In more ways than one.

AIMEE. I was attractive and Tom Gage was lonely.

MADELEINE. Well, now I know how it happened.

AIMEE. And I hope the knowledge will help you in life. Chin up, curls in place, tidy drawers, and an eye that can pick out a flea in the fur of a dog at fifty paces: that's how a woman makes her way in the world.

MADELEINE. I wish I had your fire — but I can't manage it.

AIMEE. Well, you're a goose — or a kitten by somebody's fireplace. But not Nicholas Starbuck's fireplace — not if he is what I think he is.

MADELEINE. What is that?

AIMEE. A firebrand Whiggish rebel — he and his uncle both. So I think and so I hope to prove. Pah! Our luck amazes me. Heaven will punish us if we don't make the most of it. Here's Tom Gage, whom I thought I'd never see again — commander in Boston — and willing to pay a thousand pounds for a first-class prize. Give me this, and then a year or two in Canada, add our little reserves, and I promise you we'll sail back to France in state. And there we'll bury the Marquise de Tourville, agreed? I'm like you, Madelon, plain Madame Pichot suits me too. Rich and plain. I'll marry you off to a steady barrister; we'll settle in Lyons again like pigeons come home to roost; and I'll engage two or three pretty footmen to keep the dust from settling on me.

MADELEINE. Mother, mother . . .

AIMEE. I like it, Madelon! I'm not stealing anything from you, am I? How did I ever beget this marshmallow? Well, dreaming never filled a purse. I must see that fool Weamish, and you must go on flirting violently with Mr. Nicholas. That's not too painful a task, is it?

MADELEINE. Now it is.

AIMEE. Twaddle! Worm the truth out of him. Who knows? I may be wrong about him after all. And if I can't sell him to Gage, he's yours to keep. Marry your commoner. Down with privilege! Fifteen years in America have made an egalitarian even of your mother.

SCENE THREE

(Wednesday, June 21. Morning. The WEAMISH residence, as in the first scene. JUDGE WEAMISH and CAPTAIN CUFF in conference)

CUFF. How many windmills d'you have on the island?

WEAMISH. Oh, quite a few —

CUFF. Quite a few is a slovenly answer, Judge. I've but forty men under me. Everywhere we go we're surrounded by swarms of urchins. The urchins run ahead to warn their elders, and by the time we reach a spot it's been swept clear of weapons and ammunition. But Captain Cuff can play the fox too. You wait and see.

WEAMISH. Most of the islanders are loyal, Captain. Need I remind you that a dozen of our vessels are secretly supplying General Gage and Admiral Graves, at great risk to themselves?

CUFF. What of it? You're giving me tuppence with one hand and picking my pocket with the other.

WEAMISH. Didn't the Starbucks promise to help?

CUFF. They did. But we was interrupted by that sea rescue you heard of. Brave lad, young Starbuck is; naturally, a soldier's a soldier — it's the bloody merchants I can't abide —

WEAMISH. Well —

CUFF. Now here's what I expect *you* to do, Judge —

(Enter JENNY)

JENNY. Excuse me. The French lady is here again, Mr. Weamish.

(Enter AIMEE)

AIMEE. No ceremony, please. Good morning, Judge. Ah, Captain Cuff —

CUFF. Madam —

WEAMISH. Marquise, what a pleasure to see you this morning. I hope you spent a restful night at Swain's.

AIMEE. So-so, thank you. The wind, the sea, and the seagulls kept us company.

WEAMISH. Pray sit. Jenny —

AIMEE. Thank you. No refreshments. That will be all, Jenny.

JENNY. Yes ma'am.

(*She hurries out*)

WEAMISH. And how is your daughter this sunny morning, Marquise?

AIMEE. My daughter is singing romantic ditties by the seashore, thank you. But I didn't —

WEAMISH. I have been apprised of the dreadful and thrilling event to which you were a witness yesterday.

AIMEE. Precisely what —

WEAMISH. On your first day in Sherburne! Our life, you see, is a rough one. Not a month goes by without a tragic loss at sea — weeping widows and orphans — valuable freights of blubber lost —

AIMEE. Life is a series of tempests, Judge. I —

WEAMISH. How true! And how sad! I feel you are divining the thoughts I nurtured during the night.

AIMEE. Thoughts, Judge?

WEAMISH. To distract us all from the very tempests you have named, I have decided to offer a ball in your honor this Saturday. If you would condescend — you and Mademoiselle Madeleine — to grace this soiree — it would, I assure you —

AIMEE. Let me cut you short, my dear Judge. Not to be rude — I am utterly grateful for your delicate attentions — but I came to Nantucket with an important charge. Let us talk about dancing another time.

WEAMISH. I defer to you, Marquise.

AIMEE. Captain, yesterday, very briefly, I had the pleasure of meeting you and of presenting my credentials. (*The CAPTAIN bows*) When that supposed steward was rescued from the sea, I tried as effectively as I knew how to show you my interest in this dubious figure.

CUFF. I don't follow these subtleties, madam. Supposed steward? Dubious figure? What the deuce do you mean?

AIMEE. It's simple enough. Between this castaway and the Starbucks I sensed a connection that needs to be probed.

CUFF. Between the Starbucks —

AIMEE. Do keep repeating my words after me, Captain; it can do you no harm.

WEAMISH. Extraordinary woman!

CUFF. Devils in hell! Explain yourself, Marquise; I'm a plain Briton; I'm not the man for your Frenchified mysteries.

WEAMISH. You don't know as yet, Captain Cuff, what Madame and I happen to have learned: the Starbucks are suspected.

CUFF. Suspected! God's guts! I'm down to repeating everybody's words this morning! The Starbucks suspected! The drowning steward a spy! And what am I? The buffoon in a Punch and Judy show? Weamish — damn your legal mincing — you let me rattle on about the Starbucks five minutes ago without saying a word.

WEAMISH. Not without the Marquise's —

CUFF. I'll arrest the lot of you! Everybody's suspected here!

AIMEE. Calm yourself, Captain. If you'd taken notice of my signs, this pretended steward with his silk shirt and his gold buttons would have been in our custody by now instead of resting quietly at the Starbuck's house.

WEAMISH. More acuity and less shouting, Captain.

CUFF. Y'are right, damn my tongue. I'm lessoned. Explain to me, Marquise.

AIMEE. I'm not sure of anything as yet. But we know that the rebel Congress is desperate for experienced military leaders. We know that Colonels Starbuck and Washington are acquainted. We believe that young Nicholas was implicated in a Bostonian affair in '65 —

CUFF. What affair?

WEAMISH. What is this, Marquise?

AIMEE. We *think* he was one of your so-called Sons of Liberty —

WEAMISH. Impossible!

AIMEE. One of a gang that smashed the Stamp Distributor's furniture in Boston.

WEAMISH. I'm speechless! Mr. Oliver it was — and they broke my window here that very same week! Heaven cries out —

CUFF. I'll cut his throat!

AIMEE. Gently, Captain Cuff —

CUFF. I'll cut it gently, by Lucifer's pike, but I'll cut it!

AIMEE. We also know that he shot and killed a British officer in Long Island two years ago — an officer who was trying to impress a couple of his seamen.

WEAMISH. *That*, Marquise, is known to all of us.

CUFF. Not to me, devils in hell, not to me!

WEAMISH. What can we do? Young Nick has braved the oceans from New Guinea to Labrador; he has a prompt temper. When two of his men were being forced away from him — well, Marquise, I must own — reluctantly — that the Nantucket people regard this action of Mr. Starbuck's as — how shall I put it —

AIMEE. A businesslike move?

WEAMISH. Very nearly.

CUFF. Shooting an officer is a businesslike move?

AIMEE. Gently, Captain, gently. I don't choose to lay heavy stress on this transaction, either. It might have been the impulse of a perfectly loyal subject, am I right?

WEAMISH. A loyal subject of our peculiar Nantucket — yes, Marquise. Reluctantly, yes.

CUFF. I have three arrests to make. Good day —

AIMEE. You are not arresting anyone, Captain. Not until I'm vastly more confident than I am now.

CUFF. I'm to twiddle my thumbs, am I, while your rebels bubble the King of England? The house is burning, says Captain Cuff; don't wait for the firemen; man the buckets and pour!

WEAMISH. What house is burning? You say this after our glorious victory at Charlestown?

CUFF. Judge Weamish: with all due respect, you civilians are dreamers. We got trounced on the confounded hill, what d'you call it. Y'are a fool, let a soldier tell you.

WEAMISH. Sir!

CUFF. A fool! Hang the pussyfooters!

AIMEE. Captain Cuff, gently gently will do it. Did we or did we not rout the Yankee mob?

CUFF. First of all, my dear Marquise, with due respect once more, y'are a fool to talk about a mob. Don't credit the gossip you heard in your New York mansions. That mob bled us white afore they took leave of the peninsula. Y'are a friend of General Gage's, are you? Then tell him from Captain Cuff, he knows me well enough, the fine gentleman, tell him he'd be wise to clear out of Boston altogether, for he'll never set foot on another inch of Massachusetts soil. The fop hasn't so much as a good map of the country. He pinches actresses at the playhouse while the enemy is mustering. He waits for reinforcements from England instead of peppering the rebels from cock-crow till curfew. When he does fight them, what does he do? Climbs up the confounded hill in a frontal attack, because, don't you see, the enemy is nothing but a cowardly mob, show 'em your teeth and they'll run. Well, they forgot to run. They chopped us into little pieces and strolled away at their own sweet leisure.

AIMEE (to WEAMISH). Is this true? Is it then as Mr. Starbuck suggested yesterday?

CUFF. Aha; Mr. Starbuck suggested, did he? He'll suggest from the jailhouse as of today. Without further ceremony —

AIMEE. No, Captain, I forbid it all the same.

CUFF. A Frenchwoman forbids Captain Cuff? Ha ha ha!

AIMEE. Judge!

WEAMISH. Come now, sir, no draconian measures as yet. The Starbucks have committed no illegal act, and arresting them would create a perilous unease throughout the island. The colonel is one of our selectmen this year. An old, highly regarded family, with numberless influential relations, here and in Boston.

CUFF. Pffff!

AIMEE. Judge Weamish is making several excellent points.

CUFF. When these courtesies are over, Judge, your colonies will have whistled off the King for good.

WEAMISH. You misunderstand our fundamental loyalty.

AIMEE. Are not several of the Starbucks' merchantmen tied up in Sherburne now?

WEAMISH. I daresay they are.

CUFF. Wrong. The Colonel's *Queen Bess* put in a week ago, but his other three sail are on the seas, and so, worse luck, are two sloops belonging to the nephew.

AIMEE. That still gives us a respectable hostage. Keep a discreet eye upon the *Queen Bess*, Captain. Let there be no suspicions. I engage to discover within twenty-four hours whether the Starbucks are intending to fly the coop or not. My daughter is working on young Nick; I shall attack the uncle. Never fear.

CUFF. I take my leave.

AIMEE. Don't violate your instructions, Captain; or the Governor shall hear of it.

CUFF. I shan't touch either of the Starbucks. Good day to you both.

WEAMISH. Good day, Captain. Always a —

(*CAPTAIN CUFF is gone, slamming the door*)

WEAMISH. Bear in mind, Marquise, that our Captain has reached an age when, had he been a man of any consequence, he would have had a regiment. Thoughts such as these cloud his perceptions.

AIMEE. His perceptions look singularly clear to me.

WEAMISH. Now, however, that our political affairs are running their course, I beg you, dearest lady, to take pity upon our ball this Saturday. Make history on our island, madam!

AIMEE. That is what I propose to do.

(*WEAMISH kisses her hand*)

SCENE FOUR

(Wednesday, June 21. Morning. ELIAS STARBUCK's house. HENRY WALLIS is sleeping on a couch. Beside him sits NICHOLAS, watching him, and obviously happy and excited. Enter RUTH, the maid, carrying a large tray with breakfast and coffee)

NICHOLAS. Hush. Don't wake him. Put the things down quietly. Is there a cup for me? Ah. Thanks, Ruthie.

(Exit RUTH. NICHOLAS walks about the room, looks out of a window by edging open a shutter — the shutters have been closed for WALLIS' benefit — then pulls out a letter he has clearly read several times already)

NICHOLAS *(kissing the letter)*. Did ever mistress speak more sweetly? *(He reads)* "You, Nicholas Starbuck, may, by force of arms, attack, subdue, and take all ships and other vessels belonging to the inhabitants of Great Britain. You shall bring — "

WALLIS. The pouch!

NICHOLAS. Wallis, are you awake?

WALLIS. Ah, Mr. Starbuck, it's you.

NICHOLAS *(taking his hand)*. You haven't forgotten that we spoke for a few minutes before you fell asleep again?

WALLIS. When?

NICHOLAS. Last night.

WALLIS. Yes — yes! I remember! Mr. Starbuck — you saved my life — I don't know whether I thanked you — or thanked you enough —

NICHOLAS. Nonsense!

WALLIS. Without you —

NICHOLAS. And where would *I* be without *you*?

WALLIS. Is the pouch safe?

NICHOLAS. You *have* forgotten!

WALLIS. Forgive me.

NICHOLAS. You were clutching it, half drowned you were holding on to it.

My uncle and I took it away from you. He has his letter, and I have both of mine.

WALLIS. Thank God! Where is your uncle?

NICHOLAS. In his study, meditating upon the letter. Shall I open the shutters?

WALLIS. Oh — it's daytime, is it?

NICHOLAS. As glorious a morning as I ever hope to see.

WALLIS. And I'm alive!

NICHOLAS. Brave Wallis. Raise yourself up; come, I'll help you. Set your face boldly toward the table. What do you see there?

WALLIS (*laughing*). Breakfast!

NICHOLAS. Shall I bring it to you?

WALLIS. No, I'll try to get up. Thank you for the clothes.

NICHOLAS. Try to stand, Harry.

WALLIS. Not bad. Not bad. Wait — I'll do it alone.

NICHOLAS. Good fellow.

WALLIS. Your floor's a bit unsteady, Mr. Starbuck.

NICHOLAS. But navigable, eh?

WALLIS. Navigable. Ah, the sun! the sun! But the news I carry for you — I haven't forgotten, God be praised.

NICHOLAS. Sit down. Eat. Drink.

WALLIS. Yes. I want to. Forgive me, but I'll discard manners and fling myself.

NICHOLAS. Cautiously, Wallis.

WALLIS. Yes. Good. Oh, this is a blessed day. (*NICHOLAS pours the coffee*) Thank you, thank you. There were two items in writing for you, Mr. Starbuck, and General Washington's letter for your uncle. You have all three?

NICHOLAS. All three. Eat, Wallis, eat. But did you say *General* Washington?

WALLIS. He was promoted the day before he wrote that letter. But he had premonitions and intimations, you understand. A Mr. Reed is his secretary. Most capable. Some of the letters were written in advance. There'll be lively actions, Mr. Starbuck, sudden decisions and prompt executions.

NICHOLAS. And we must be sudden and prompt enough, by God, to keep ahead of them. Eat, Wallis, eat and drink. What else?

WALLIS. Your cousin Mr. Pigeon.

NICHOLAS. Yes! What does he say? Did he reach Philadelphia in time?

WALLIS. In good time; Mr. Pigeon is now commissary general for Massachusetts —

NICHOLAS. And will purchase — ?

WALLIS. And will purchase whatever you choose to capture, sir. No questions asked. He'll purchase doilies for the Army if doilies is what you take at sea. We were sitting in a private room at the City — that's the tavern of our true-hearted Whigs when the speechifying has made them thirsty — and he was laughing till the tears rolled from his eyes and his belly bobbed like a lifebuoy. Doilies and diapers, he kept repeating, Cousin Pigeon will pay for Massachusetts! You can't miss, Mr. Starbuck.

NICHOLAS. If they don't find him out and tar and feather him, the villain! But he gave you nothing in writing?

WALLIS. Pigeon don't put anything in writing except birthday wishes to his mother.

NICHOLAS. But is Fillmore going to believe this in Salem? Verbal promises reported at second hand?

WALLIS. The question occurred to me. Pigeon agreed to send a trusted messenger to Salem; the man will tell Fillmore what I have told you. Nothing in writing.

NICHOLAS. That will have to do. And Pigeon himself — what are his terms?

WALLIS. Ten percent; plus an eighth share in Mr. Davis' chocolate mill.

NICHOLAS. An eighth? You didn't agree, did you? A full eighth?

WALLIS. I argued; ordered more rum; but Mr. Pigeon is quite above rum. It was an eighth or nothing. "Young Nick ain't the only swashbuckler in the Atlantic," says he. I must report honestly, Mr. Starbuck.

NICHOLAS. You must indeed. An eighth it shall be. I need him more than he needs me, damn his blubbery soul!

WALLIS. There you are.

NICHOLAS. And a wise man knows how to give in order to take. The pieces are falling into place, Wallis! Christ — if we'd lost you yesterday! One missing nail will bring an empire down. (*He takes out another letter from a pocket*) Do you know what's written in this?

WALLIS. I know it's from Mr. Davis, of course, and I know it concerns Mrs. Applegate — that's all.

NICHOLAS. I'll tell you. Wait. (*He goes to the door, looks into the next room, and comes back. Then he pulls close to WALLIS*) Davis writes that Mrs. Applegate does have the power to sell. To sell every blessed acre they own at Concord.

WALLIS. That's good. Is Mr. Applegate still here?

NICHOLAS. More than ever; very thick with Judge Weamish and Captain Cuff; and offers snuff to the redcoats on Duke Street.

WALLIS. What redcoats?

NICHOLAS. Right — you don't know that we are entertaining the British army. I fancy Tom Gage is thinking he might seize Nantucket. Now. Davis tells me that dear Mrs. Applegate is suffering many vexations alone at Concord as the wife of an escaped Tory. One or two more frights and she'll sell for ten shillings in the pound. Davis has her confidence and is willing to buy for me when the time is ripe. You, Wallis, shall make it ripe.

WALLIS. How?

NICHOLAS. You'll go to Concord and tell the good people there that Mr. Applegate, let me see, Mr. Applegate is compiling secret lists of Whigs for Gage's benefit; trying to muster a Loyalist militia. What else? Yes: acting as go-between to supply the British from Nantucket. The fact is, they *are* being supplied, no one can deny it.

WALLIS. I'll do my best. And after Concord — on to Salem to see Mr. Fillmore?

NICHOLAS. Right. I'll give you a letter.

WALLIS. When will *you* be crossing to the mainland, Mr. Starbuck?

NICHOLAS. That's for my uncle to decide. For the moment no one's allowed to leave the island. But if the *Enterprise* is returning for you this Saturday —

WALLIS. It is without fail.

NICHOLAS. I *think* we'll go with you, Wallis. A little voice tells me so. And if we do — and when we get to the mainland — Henry, how would you like the command of a brig?

WALLIS. Mr. Starbuck!

NICHOLAS. Trust me. You see but a part of my machine, you can't see it all.

WALLIS. I don't ask —

NICHOLAS. You don't need to. I'll tell you this much, however: Ben Fillmore is going to fit me out a *dozen* brigs on the strength of cousin Pigeon's promise; and you shall command one of them.

WALLIS. I'm overwhelmed.

NICHOLAS. And after that, Wallis, the world is ours for the plucking. We'll whip the king home. We'll cut the cables. We'll make a king of our own, why not? And those of us who have served — you, me, my uncle — *we'll* bestow the titles and parcel out the land!

WALLIS (*laughing*). I like that! You shall be Earl of Sherburne!

NICHOLAS. Agreed! And you Sir Henry Wallis! Knighted, not by a king of Hanover, but by the United Provinces of America! Is your belly filled, Wallis, or shall I call for another half-dozen rolls?

WALLIS. All's well in the hold, Mr. Starbuck. You make me dizzy.

NICHOLAS. Hush — I think I hear my uncle stirring. Not a word, Wallis.

WALLIS. Not in my dreams!

(*Enter STARBUCK, grave*)

STARBUCK (*stretching out his hand*). Happy to see you up and well again, Mr. Wallis.

WALLIS. Happy to be alive, Colonel, thanks to Mr. Starbuck.

NICHOLAS. Enough of that.

STARBUCK. We're deeply in debt to you, Henry. Impossible to think of you as our "agent." As anything except a most precious friend.

WALLIS. I don't know what to say. Mine is a family of humble sailors —

NICHOLAS. Uncle — are you free to tell us what was in that letter? I can't help being miserably curious about it.

STARBUCK. Before we talk about letters — no one recognized you last night, Henry — *I* wouldn't have recognized you! But now we'd best be careful. Stay within as much as possible, until we all take wing from Nantucket.

NICHOLAS. Take wing; music to my ears! The letter, Uncle!

WALLIS. Perhaps I should withdraw.

STARBUCK. By no means. You told us last night that the *Enterprise* will be here again three days from now.

WALLIS. Yes, Colonel. Captain Fleming will bring her round the island on

Saturday and drop anchor off the south coast between Weweeder and Nobadeer Pond. He'll look for signals from us all day.

NICHOLAS. Are we off, Uncle?

STARBUCK. We're off, come what may. Saturday at sunset.

NICHOLAS. At last!

STARBUCK. Obed Coffin will row us aboard. He's a man I trust like a brother. We have orders to be at Cambridge before Washington's own arrival.

NICHOLAS. Washington in Cambridge? Come, sir, the news; I'll enlist with the redcoats if you keep your secrets another minute!

STARBUCK. That would be ungrateful of you, seeing he mentions you in his letter.

NICHOLAS. How does he know me?

STARBUCK. By reputation, you dog! He personally approved your privateering commission. When the time comes to build a fleet of our own, he'll call you home again.

NICHOLAS. And you, Uncle, what about you?

STARBUCK (*takes out the letter*). Where was it? Ah. "Your bold nephew" —

NICHOLAS. Uncle! To the point!

STARBUCK (*laughing*). Can't I interest you in my bold nephew? Very well. Uncle Starbuck is to accompany General Schuyler into Canada.

NICHOLAS. Canada again!

STARBUCK. Yes. We took it away from France, and now we must take it away from England. Wait. 'Tis a longish letter. "Your bold nephew" — no, that's not the part. Here it is. "Our capture of Fort Ticonderoga on the 26th of May has encouraged the Congress to strike boldly into Canada. General Schuyler has been appointed to lead the northern expedition. He will not pause until Montreal and Quebec have fallen into our hands and our Canadian brethren are embraced into the common cause. Your task, my dear friend, will be to assist General Schuyler as his brigadier."

NICHOLAS. Wallis! Did you hear that?

WALLIS. I had an inkling —

STARBUCK. "I entreat you to meet me at Cambridge in the first days of July, for I may as well make known to you here and now what you shall undoubtedly be reading in the gazettes, to wit that the Congress has seen fit to entrust me, for the time being, with the defence of our sacred interests. I am proceeding immediately to Cambridge to take command of the army surrounding Boston."

NICHOLAS. This should be sung by a choir, d'you hear?

(*He embraces STARBUCK*)

WALLIS. May I offer my congratulations, sir?

(*STARBUCK takes his hand*)

STARBUCK. Thank you, Henry. Think of it, young Nick — you at sea, I on land, God in heaven, and Washington before Boston!

NICHOLAS (*laughing*). Sound, ye trumpets!

STARBUCK. For the eighth day of Creation. Oh my friends, a nation from our loins!

WALLIS (*who has been facing one of the windows*). Somebody's coming!
(*STARBUCK and NICHOLAS turn quickly to the window*)
STARBUCK. The Marquise's daughter!
NICHOLAS. Madeleine!
STARBUCK. She stopped. She's hesitating. Why so shy? I shouldn't be
surprised — by Jove, she's anxious about you — modesty at grips with —
look! how charming!
NICHOLAS. Rubbish! But she *is* coming towards the house. Isn't she
beautiful?
STARBUCK. We sail on Saturday, Nick.
NICHOLAS. That's three times twenty-four hours! Gentlemen — you've
business to discuss — and if you haven't, invent it — in my uncle's study —
and tell Ruthie I shall open the door myself.
(*STARBUCK and WALLIS laugh*)
STARBUCK. Come on, Henry; I'll explain who this beauty is.
WALLIS. Have I not seen her before?
NICHOLAS. Away, away! (*The two leave, laughing. NICHOLAS gazes out
the window*) Is this for me? Daughter of a marchioness. Nicholas, "bold
nephew" —
(*There is a knock at the door; NICHOLAS vanishes; the stage is empty; then
NICHOLAS reappears, escorting MADELEINE into the room; MADELEINE
is manifestly agitated*)
MADELEINE. Might someone have seen me from one of the houses?
NICHOLAS. Pray calm yourself. I doubt it. But what if someone had?
MADELEINE. No — they musn't. Mr. Starbuck —
NICHOLAS. Nicholas —
MADELEINE. Nicholas — what will you think of me? But — your action
yesterday — it was so beautiful — terrifying and beautiful — and I needed
to know — are you well? But I see you are!
NICHOLAS. The swim braced me. I sneezed a little only to alarm you — and
to give me the pretext I wanted to allay your fears in person this afternoon.
You've forestalled me.
MADELEINE. I'm shameless!
NICHOLAS. You're divine.
MADELEINE. And the steward — ?
NICHOLAS. Slept as if never to wake again. But here you see the ruins of his
breakfast.
MADELEINE. Is he grateful? Does he know?
NICHOLAS. Oh yes — but, my dear — (*softly*) my dearest Madeleine —
what I did yesterday is an everyday occurrence among us. We live from the
sea, and alas we are apt to die in the sea. These rescues are like helping
someone from an overturned coach in Paris.
MADELEINE. And yet, who else threw himself into these monstrous waves?
Don't say any more; I shall believe in you, Nicholas.
NICHOLAS. Forever?
MADELEINE. Forever? What do you mean?

NICHOLAS. Madeleine — I am a man — I cannot be near so much beauty — such grace — so much tender regard — without saying "Forever." (*He takes her in his arms. She half resists*)
MADELEINE. This is not why I came — believe me — do believe me. (*He kisses her*) — Nicholas — (*She kisses him*)
NICHOLAS. Madeleine — we have met only three times —
MADELEINE (*recoiling*). You see, you despise me!
NICHOLAS. Angel of heaven! *My* presumption is what makes me tremble. You will think me rash — brutal — to ask you — after so brief an acquaintance — but war is impatient . . . Would you be a sailor's bride — take your share of my hardships — go with me to the end of the world —
MADELEINE. I would, Nicholas, and I say it because it can never be. I came here only to warn you — please don't misunderstand —
NICHOLAS. Sit beside me. You're trembling, my angel.
MADELEINE. I don't know what you are, Nicholas, you and your uncle — Tories or Whigs —
NICHOLAS (*surprised*). Oh?
MADELEINE. But I trust you utterly, my instinct tells me you are better men than your stupid judge and that nasty captain —
NICHOLAS (*smiling*). I hope so.
MADELEINE. If you are a Tory, I'm alarmed about nothing at all — and then you must forgive a silly girl, a stranger, for meddling to no purpose. But if you are Whigs, Nicholas, *active* Whigs, beware, I beg you.
NICHOLAS. How is it you know so much, Madeleine?
MADELEINE. I have been hearing rumors, tales . . .
NICHOLAS. Our tavern's a fine place for that! But rest assured. I know all about these suspicions. Loyalists are not exempt. Everybody is watched and everybody is watching.
MADELEINE. True. But with you — there is a difference.
NICHOLAS. Why? (*MADELEINE hesitates*) Why is there a difference?
MADELEINE (*quickly, whispering*). Don't trust my mother — she — she gossips — (*She rises and tries to run away — but NICHOLAS stops her*) Let me leave —
NICHOLAS. Not with tears in your eyes. Don't go yet — come back to me — gently — calm yourself. (*He makes her sit down; she is crying a little; he puts his hands on her cheeks*) Calm yourself, lovely, kind Madeleine.
MADELEINE. Did you hear what I said?
NICHOLAS. Of course I did. I'll not trust your mother, I promise. She's fond of company, lively conversation, and a bit of gossip out of turn. I know. I shall speak to her only about us, Madeleine and Nicholas. (*He pronounces his own name in the French manner*) Is not my French pretty? Nicholas et Madeleine. Or will you become simple Madelyn in our homely English?
MADELEINE. It can never be, Nicholas, never never never —
NICHOLAS. Does the barrier between us frighten you so?
MADELEINE. Barrier? Ah —
NICHOLAS. And do you know so little about this America of ours? Between

you and me I recognize neither moat nor wall. Here we begin fresh, as in a new Garden of Eden.

MADELEINE. I know. But you —

NICHOLAS. Wait! Don't answer yet. Will you listen to me a little while longer?

MADELEINE. Of course.

NICHOLAS. You land among us almost by accident. You discover our unpolished seamen and farmers, so different from the elegance you have known. No fine carriages, no diamonds —

MADELEINE. How wrong you are —

NICHOLAS. But you haven't probed beneath the surface. Let me tell you my story. When I'm done, you shall lead me proudly to the fearsome Marquise, and she shall give her consent.

MADELEINE. Never, my precious, never.

NICHOLAS. We are Whigs, Madeleine.

MADELEINE (*joyful*). It couldn't be otherwise.

NICHOLAS. The man I rescued yesterday was our agent.

MADELEINE. And you knew it?

NICHOLAS. Of course. We were expecting him — with important messages from Philadelphia. They proved even more important than we thought. I love you, Madeleine. I will tell you my deepest secrets.

MADELEINE. No . . .

NICHOLAS. We have been summoned, my uncle and I, to meet the new commander-in-chief at Cambridge.

MADELEINE. To do God's work, Nicholas!

NICHOLAS. Amen. I am nothing now, Madeleine; I own a mere two ships, but the doors are opening to me. Look. This is a precious document. By virtue of it your Nicholas is now a privateer.

MADELEINE. What is a privateer?

NICHOLAS. A pirate!

MADELEINE. I understand — a *corsaire* — for your people.

NICHOLAS. Yes. But this is only the first link. At Salem a great man is waiting for me. He wants to equip the fleet which is to sail under my command. My private share of the booty is an entire fifth, Madeleine, nothing to be sneered at. But now comes my second man. A gentleman in a high place in the army, who undertakes to purchase whatever I capture, sight unseen, lock, stock, and barrel. Do you follow me?

MADELEINE. I think so.

NICHOLAS. My third man is a banker in Philadelphia. The moment I have got my first two bargains in my pocket, he will advance me, what shall I call it? a majestic sum of money. And then —

MADELEINE. You will be a nabob.

NICHOLAS. We shall see! A year ago, when the Parliament ruined our sea trade, I joined in an expedition against the Shawnees, deep in the West —

MADELEINE. Did you kill many Indians, Nicholas?

NICHOLAS. I have killed better men than Indians.

MADELEINE. Yes, you are brave.

NICHOLAS. Though they have nearly killed me more than once! At Niagara Falls — but that's another story. In Virginia I met a fascinating person — a Judge Henderson — I can't tell you all the particulars now, Madeleine, but they're magnificent! Henderson bought land from the savages for next to nothing — a few pound sterling — a sack of trinkets — plenty of rum, too! More land than your French king possesses. Tell me, how well do you know our country?

MADELEINE. I'm very ignorant.

NICHOLAS. Have you heard of the Kentucky, the Ohio, the Cumberland?

MADELEINE. Yes. They are mountains and provinces.

NICHOLAS. They are also rivers. With land in between. A country unto itself. We've given it a noble name — Transylvania — and in that country Henderson is holding a splendid tract for me. No one knows about this, Madeleine, except you.

MADELEINE. Not even your uncle?

NICHOLAS. I should say not! Not about this nor about anything else I have told you. He has more important concerns. General Starbuck is going to lead an army. You needn't be ashamed of us, you see. But where was I?

MADELEINE. Your land — and the *savages* —

NICHOLAS. I am entrusting you with my secrets, Madeleine.

MADELEINE. They will die with me.

NICHOLAS. Land! And more land! We'll be lords! Your princes of the blood will come and kiss our hands. But Henderson wants hard cash on the table. And that is why I forged that long beautiful chain.

MADELEINE. You're extraordinary.

NICHOLAS. With special beauties in it — an estate at Concord — a chocolate mill . . . But we'll not live in Massachusetts, you and I. Virginia is the place for us.

MADELEINE. Why?

NICHOLAS. You'll feel at home there. They will treat you as you deserve. You'll be waited upon by a retinue of glistening blacks! Oh Madeleine, I've been prating like a fool this half hour — sordid mercantile affairs, but how else could you learn who and what we are? I love you. You are as beautiful —

MADELEINE. As the chain?

NICHOLAS (*tenderly*). The chain is to bind you with.

MADELEINE. Nicholas — I'm a little dizzy —

NICHOLAS. And I'm a boor! I haven't even offered you —

MADELEINE. No no — only a glass of water.

NICHOLAS. Here.

MADELEINE. Thank you. Such marvelous stories — only in America can one hear such stories. I feel so old. Let me go back now to my little inn, Nicholas — don't speak anymore about — it — and us — for the time being —

NICHOLAS. I've babbled and babbled.

MADELEINE. No — it was good to hear —

NICHOLAS. Was it? Was it truly? Madeleine, I loved you the mo—

MADELEINE. No — you promised —

NICHOLAS. I did — for the time being.

MADELEINE. Will you remember the one important thing I said?

NICHOLAS. Which one, Madeleine?

MADELEINE. Not to trust —

NICHOLAS. Your —

MADELEINE. Anyone.

(*She leaves. NICHOLAS watches her from the window*)

NICHOLAS. Damn my tongue! Did I fall into a trap? Nonsense! Though I worship her, that was love in her blue eyes too, and love on her thirsty lips, as sure as fish can swim. Uncle! Wallis! Let's resume!

SCENE FIVE

(*Thursday, June 22. Morning. A lane in Sherburne. Sunny day. MADELEINE is sitting on a bench. She is deep in thought. COLONEL STARBUCK enters. He is walking slowly, reading a book with great attention. He stops, struck by a passage, and, lifting his head to reflect upon it, he sees MADELEINE. For a few moments he looks at her — she has not seen him — with evident admiration. He hesitates to intrude on her, but finally decides he will*)

STARBUCK. Mademoiselle.

MADELEINE. Colonel Starbuck! Forgive me, I didn't see you. (*She gives him her hand*)

STARBUCK. I was loth to disturb you in the very good company of your thoughts.

MADELEINE. My thoughts today are like unpleasant guests in the house.

STARBUCK. I'm sorry to hear you say so, on such a fine morning.

MADELEINE. It is a fine morning, isn't it. Will you sit by me? No — you are undoubtedly on your way to a political meeting.

STARBUCK. Not in the least. I was reading — strolling — raising my hat to my neighbors . . . I will accept your invitation.

(*She smiles; he sits down*)

MADELEINE. What is your book, Colonel? I know! A treatise on fortifying exposed harbors.

STARBUCK. No. Guess again.

MADELEINE. The poems of some refined and ailing gentlewoman of Connecticut.

STARBUCK. No.

MADELEINE. I give up.

STARBUCK. A manifesto.

MADELEINE. Ah, that's dangerous.

STARBUCK. More than you think. It came in the same bottom that brought you to Nantucket the day before yesterday.

MADELEINE. Come, tell me what it is.

STARBUCK. Are you not afraid of seditious literature?

MADELEINE. As a Frenchwoman I am immune.

STARBUCK. Ah, you are lucky to be the citizen of an old, stable nation. I believe the French have not engaged in civic broils since — let me see — when Louis XIV was a boy — and then the tumult was quickly settled. We must be a singularly restless people.

MADELEINE. Because you don't know how to be slaves.

STARBUCK. So writes my author, Mr. Jefferson.

MADELEINE. Read to me, Colonel. I am surprisingly tolerant and discreet.

STARBUCK. Still, remember that a man needn't subscribe to what he reads. A man may read the words of an enemy in order the better to foil him.

MADELEINE (laughing). I understand.

STARBUCK (leafing through the book). Here's some passable rhetoric. "The common feelings of human nature must be surrendered up before his Majesty's subjects here can be persuaded to believe that they hold their political existence at the will of a British Parliament. Shall these governments be dissolved, their property annihilated, and their people reduced to a state of nature, at the imperious breath of a body of men whom they never saw, in whom they never confided, and over whom they have no powers of punishment or removal, let their crimes against the American public be ever so great? Can any one reason be assigned why one hundred and sixty thousand electors in the island of Great Britain should give law to four millions in the States of America, every individual of whom is equal to every individual of them in virtue, in understanding, and in bodily strength? Were this to be admitted, instead of being a free people, as we have hitherto supposed and mean to continue ourselves, we should suddenly be found the slaves not of one but of one hundred and sixty thousand tyrants."

MADELEINE. Ah, I like that! Who is this flaming orator? Will you confess that he is a friend of yours? Why not? An enemy of the state might have been one's friend in the days of innocence.

STARBUCK. It is God's truth that I don't know the man.

MADELEINE. Do you think he is in jail?

STARBUCK. No; for I've been told that he is presently a delegate in Philadelphia. And were I a rebel of his complexion, were I, I would embrace him for these words.

MADELEINE. You show a fine sense, Colonel, in the estimate of your opponents. What else does your interesting firebrand say?

STARBUCK. Many wicked things — oh, if I were the king, I should not sleep easy until I did see Mr. Jefferson in fetters. For example: "By an act passed in the fifth year of the reign of his late Majesty, King George the Second, an American subject is forbidden to make a hat for himself of the fur which he has taken, perhaps, on his own soil — an instance of despotism to which no parallel can be produced in the most arbitrary ages of British history."

MADELEINE. Stop! Here I think your Mr. Henderson begins to foam at the mouth! What? Not to be allowed to make your own hat is a piece of brutality without parallel?

STARBUCK. I shouldn't have read you this passage. It is followed by a weightier one on the manufacture of iron.

MADELEINE. No, no more. Your hero must be permitted at once to sew his own beaver hat, whereupon he will turn into as good a Tory as — yourself.

STARBUCK. Well, he does allow himself to be carried away now and then. However, I beg you, Mademoiselle, to listen to one more passage.

MADELEINE. Very well.

STARBUCK. "The abolition of domestic slavery is the great object of desire in those colonies where it was, unhappily, introduced in their infant state. But previous to the enfranchisement of the slaves we have, it is necessary to exclude all further importations from Africa. Yet our repeated attempts to effect this, by prohibitions and by imposing duties which might amount to a prohibition, have been hitherto defeated by his Majesty's negative, thus preferring the immediate advantages of a few British corsairs to the lasting interests of the American States and the rights of human nature, deeply wounded by this infamous practice." Does this not touch you? "This infamous practice." Such words are quite beyond faction — we'll say no more about the beaver hats.

MADELEINE. Had you the opportunity, wouldn't you engage in the slave trade yourself, Colonel Starbuck?

STARBUCK. I — in the slave trade? I would die — no — I would *kill* — before I would let a man be handled like a bale of merchandise.

MADELEINE. But what of the pleasure of being waited on by a band of glistening blacks?

STARBUCK (*deeply grieved*). Is this you speaking, Mademoiselle?

(*MADELEINE places a reassuring hand on STARBUCK's arm*)

MADELEINE. God forbid. (*She pauses*) I was quoting your nephew.

STARBUCK (*smiling*). So *that* was the subject of your conversation yesterday — the slave trade!

MADELEINE. Or rather, trade in general. Nicholas is very gifted that way.

STARBUCK. Indeed he is. But give me leave to assure you that, like myself, Nicholas would raise his tent in Muscovy or turn heathen before he would engage in the buying and selling of slaves.

MADELEINE (*she is close to tears and replies in a whisper*). I am not so sure. (*They sit silent for a while. Then, impulsively, MADELEINE takes a pencil and a scrap of paper out of her purse, and writes a few words*)

MADELEINE. Please give him this for me. Oh, you may read it. I'm not so eloquent as your author.

STARBUCK. Is that all?

MADELEINE (*low*). Yes.

STARBUCK. Nicholas is one of our best, Madeleine. A plain dealer and a gallant fighter. He lost father and mother when he was a boy. Perhaps he wants the softer counsels of a woman to complete him as as man. But he is generous, quick-witted, exuberant in imagination. We shall need men like him. They will be our especial glory.

MADELEINE. Or your particular downfall.

STARBUCK (*downcast*). No. It must not be. You don't know him, Madeleine.

(*He tries to return the scrap of paper to her; she refuses with a gesture, and moves quickly away.*)

SCENE SIX

(*Thursday, June 22. Late afternoon. Swain's Tavern. AIMEE and MADELEINE are alone*)

AIMEE. I don't know how long I can keep that brute of a captain from arresting them.

MADELEINE. Wouldn't the islanders riot if he tried?

AIMEE. That's what I and Weamish told him. But I'm not sure I believe it myself. What a blow if he catches them before I do! Hang it, I'll not have an English bully get the better of Aimée Pichot. Not while I've got a set of teeth in my mouth. More or less.

MADELEINE. What have you found out so far, mother? Are they rebels or loyalists?

AIMEE. Rebels at heart without a doubt. But Gage is not interested in hearts. What I need is palpable mischief; a plan to join the Whig army; a plot to seize Nantucket; smuggling of arms; anything. I have an idea. Why don't you bewitch the uncle while I tackle the nephew?

MADELEINE. Why?

AIMEE. Older men are more susceptible. It'll turn his head when he sees a pretty young girl fluttering about him.

MADELEINE. You're better looking than I am, mother.

AIMEE. I was. God what a girl I was when I kept jail in Lyon. But I've lost my looks — some of my looks. What I've kept, though, is blood and guts — and that's more important with a man, when all's said and done. You're too mousy, Madeleine. You've had two days — a doll like you — and what have you accomplished?

MADELEINE. Oh, I don't know. Nicholas Starbuck proposed to me.

AIMEE. Very amusing. Yes, I think I'll unleash myself at him, and have you nibble at the uncle.

MADELEINE. I'm not joking, mother.

(*AIMEE looks at her*)

AIMEE. God strike me! Nick Starbuck — *proposed* to you? That's all? When? What happened? Where? Why?

MADELEINE. I suppose he likes me. I think he likes my noble lineage too.

AIMEE. A miracle has happened! Suddenly the girl's an expert! Come here, Madelon! (*She hugs MADELEINE*) You'll make your fortune after all. I take back the mousy. Tell me all about it, and don't leave out the erotic details, you naughty baggage!

MADELEINE. Well, he wants to marry me.

AIMEE. When did he propose? Where?

MADELEINE. What does it matter? We talked for a long time — he was very wild — very eloquent — but of course my rank made him keep his distance — most of the time.

AIMEE. What did you discover about him? Can we deliver him to Gage?

MADELEINE. We didn't discuss the political situation, mother.

AIMEE. The girl's a sensualist! What are you in this miserable island for?

MADELEINE. I discovered that Mr. Starbuck is a man with a very large future.

AIMEE. A firing squad is not a future.

MADELEINE. I'm not so sure about the firing squad. He has a very keen mind for business, mother. I wish you'd been there to listen to his projects. A fleet under his command; huge tracts of land in the West; a chocolate mill; shiny slaves; bankers urging loans and credits upon him — my head was spinning I tell you. And I kept thinking how much you'd have enjoyed it all.

AIMEE. Why was he giving you this inventory?

MADELEINE. To convince the daughter of Madame de Tourville that she wouldn't be taking a dreadful tumble down the ladder.

AIMEE. He may have been bragging.

MADELEINE. I had confirmations.

AIMEE. What confirmations?

MADELEINE. That's my secret.

AIMEE. Keep your secret! But are you sure? You're not being a simpleton — or imposing on your own mother?

MADELEINE. I am sure, mother, a hundred times sure.

AIMEE. Madeleine, this is serious. Stupendously serious. A fleet under his command. And then that cock-and-bull steward of theirs. You'd best tell me your secret. Out with it, hussy. What passed between you and Nicholas?

MADELEINE. I allowed him to kiss me once.

AIMEE. Thank you, Miss Impertinence. I'm to conclude that the Starbucks are good only for trading and kissing. Eh?

MADELEINE. If they are good for anything else, that's for you to discover.

AIMEE. By putting *you* to the question, miss. Or better yet, by striking at once. The longer I look at you, the more I'm tempted to take the risk. You're transparent, my girl.

MADELEINE. Don't be rash, mother. Your guess might be dreadfully wrong. And besides — (*she hesitates*) don't make me your enemy.

AIMEE. Aha, the little spitfire is in love! You accepted him, did you?

MADELEINE. No.

AIMEE. You refused him?

MADELEINE. Yes.

AIMEE. Why?

MADELEINE. A rebel, mother, whom you intend to deliver to Gage?

AIMEE. A rebel with a fleet, and land in the West, and confirmations, is no rebel until I've made up my mind. I will strike at once, that's settled, but which way? Here's an ambitious dog proposing to you; a man the government fears like a hundred Turks; a wizard in business. What shall we tell him when he proposes a second time?

MADELEINE. You're a whirlwind, mother! One moment we're jailing Nicholas and the next we're marrying him. I say let's leave the island. No plots, no machinations this time. Please, mother. You'll make up in Canada for the few wretched pounds you sacrificed here.

AIMEE. So anxious! You really must know a great deal! I ought to ship the Starbucks to Boston at dawn tomorrow and produce you there as a witness. You and your secret. I assure you there's nothing wretched about a thousand pounds. And I'll thank you not to threaten your own mother. On the other hand, aren't we missing the larger landscape? To hear Captain Cuff talk, the Yankees are not the sheep we've been told they are. And the Starbucks prove him right. There must be thousands of these sturdy rogues arming up and down the continent. Providence may have placed the uncle and nephew in our path to show us we were about to commit a terrible sin.

MADELEINE. But what about your former lover?

AIMEE. Who's that?

MADELEINE. General Gage.

AIMEE. What about him?

MADELEINE. Would it be quite correct to betray him?

AIMEE. Absolutely correct. He's a man of the world.

MADELEINE. But I don't want to marry Mr. Starbuck.

AIMEE. That's impossible.

MADELEINE. Why?

AIMEE. He's brave and handsome, and he's a revolutionary. Don't tell me that's against him. I hope I can read my own daughter. You're a rebel yourself, you've never fooled me, fear of your mother is all that's kept you in line.

MADELEINE. And yet I will not marry him.

AIMEE. I haven't yet decided that you should. I need time to think. Thank God we can live without Montreal, where I must be dull Madame Pichot again. We're free, Madeleine. Let's look at this Nicholas together.

MADELEINE. I'm not marrying him, mother.

AIMEE. Why not? What happened? What's wrong with him?

MADELEINE. He's too pretty for me. I hate men with small mouths.

AIMEE. The girl's a lunatic! One minute you talk like a woman of sense and experience; the next, you babble nonsense that would shame an infant! What's a small mouth got to do with the size of what counts?

MADELEINE. I don't care.

AIMEE. Madeleine my child — I love you dearly, and I forgive you your dubious origins — but one of these days you and I must part company. Gold turns to clay in your hands. You'll become a bad influence on me when I'm older and weaker and can't put up a fight. Mr. Swain!

SWAIN (appearing). Madam desires?

AIMEE. A bowl of grog, if you please! (SWAIN vanishes) Young Starbuck proposes to you; you refuse him; but you'll throttle your mother to protect him. I must ponder this mystery for a while. (SWAIN reappears with the order) Thank you, Mr. Swain. (SWAIN leaves) And make, as you say, my own discoveries.

SCENE SEVEN

(*Thursday, June 22. Night. A beach on the south shore of Nantucket. In the back, we see a so-called "stage" — that is to say a small house used by the cod fishermen of Nantucket. The sound of the ocean surf nearby. Enter the STARBUCKS and OBED COFFIN, who is carrying a light*)

STARBUCK. This is the place I have chosen. Saturday at sunset we'll flash our signal to the *Enterprise* from here. Let's hope the weather holds.

OBED. I've got a feeling it will, Colonel. My bones usually tell me three days in advance if there's a storm stirring up.

NICHOLAS. Well, Obed, two days of your bones is all we need, so don't let them fool us.

STARBUCK. When shall we see our island again, Nick?

NICHOLAS. When indeed?

STARBUCK. This particular sea-wind and this especial smell of the heather, that grows nowhere else in America. I feel by anticipation the ache I shall feel when we are gone.

NICHOLAS (*to OBED*). Don't forget plenty of pitch for our signal.

OBED. I've got a barrel of it in the house, sir.

NICHOLAS. Good.

STARBUCK. With God's help we shall reach our destination on the eve of the Sabbath — in time to kneel in church.

NICHOLAS (*laughing*). Uncle, for once I'll kneel with you. I expect we'll have something to be thankful for.

OBED. I forgot to ask. Will you be taking a heap of baggage? Because if you are, I'll ask my brother Tim to help row us out.

STARBUCK. We'll have next to nothing. Better to arrive on the mainland naked than to be met by the Captain's men carrying out a couple of trunks.

OBED. We'll guard your house when you're gone, Colonel. Let them try to touch it!

STARBUCK. Thanks, Obed. But don't allow violence and bloodshed, God forbid, on account of our house. If the war goes against us, it will be lost anyhow.

NICHOLAS. Have we seen to everything, Uncle?

STARBUCK. I think so. This is a fine sheltered beach.

OBED. We'll haul my boat to the water's edge on Saturday afternoon. You'll not waste a minute.

NICHOLAS. It's getting chilly. Hey — who's this?

OBED. Somebody racing our way. What shall we do?

STARBUCK. Somebody who knows we're here. (*He pulls out a pistol*) Stand still and leave him to me.

VOICE. Colonel! Mr. Starbuck!

STARBUCK. It's Mamack!

(*Enter MAMACK*)

MAMACK. They've arrested Mr. Wallis!

(*He falls on the sand out of breath*)

NICHOLAS. Confound them! Arrested Wallis!

STARBUCK. Catch your breath, Mamack, and tell us what happened.

MAMACK. I'll try — in a minute — I been lookin' for you high and low — left my horse half a mile away! They arrested Mr. Wallis right outside your house, Colonel, I guess he was taking the air, being as it was dark — I hear that four redcoats come up to him and drug him away.

OBED. Damn their eyes! They'll pay for this!

MAMACK. There's worse to come. The Captain got three or four men to recognize Mr. Wallis.

NICHOLAS. Damnation!

STARBUCK. This is a blow.

NICHOLAS. Tupper, Folger, Rotch — I'll take my oath they were the first to play Judas.

MAMACK. You say right, Mr. Starbuck; and Abe Myrick too.

NICHOLAS. We'll pickle them to our taste before this war is over.

OBED. Amen.

MAMACK. The town's huffing mad right now, I tell you. As soon as word go out that somebody was arrested off o' your doorstep, Colonel, people start comin' out into the streets. There's a crowd in front of the jail, another one in front of the Judge's house, and another one by your house to see nobody touches you.

NICHOLAS. What next, Uncle?

STARBUCK. Well, they've got Wallis. And who is Wallis? Our business agent. Where's the crime in that?

NICHOLAS. Yes — but why did we conceal him? Why, when I pulled him out of the sea — why didn't I cry "Wallis, dear old business agent"?

STARBUCK. Because our business affairs are private. I hope we've a right to keep our affairs to ourselves.

OBED. Sounds reasonable to me. They're bound to release Wallis tomorrow.

NICHOLAS. Unless they whip or beat the truth out of him.

STARBUCK. I don't think the Captain feels safe enough to misuse a prisoner. Back to town, men. We must pay the Judge a visit.

NICHOLAS. Right! Cuff wouldn't have struck without Weamish's connivance. We'll make our fop of a judge sweat a little.

MAMACK. I hear hoofbeats. Wait.

(*He hurries out*)

NICHOLAS. What now?

STARBUCK. Perhaps the Captain has come to arrest us too.

(*He pulls out his pistol again. OBED draws his knife*)

NICHOLAS. I'll twist his head about his neck if he tries.

(*MAMACK returns*)

MAMACK. It's the lady in the chaise! Coming from 'Sconset way!

STARBUCK. What lady?

MAMACK. The French one, the older one — old Moses is driving her!

NICHOLAS. Christ! Madeleine warned me not to trust the mother. Snuff the light, Obed! A pox on her! Wallis arrested — all of us confabulating at the seashore at night —

STARBUCK. Steady, steady. Leave this to me. (*He advances*) Who goes there? Stand and answer ere you take another step.

AIMEE (*entering*). Don't shoot, whoever you are — this is the foreign lady — ah — Colonel Starbuck! What a heavenly surprise!

STARBUCK. The surprise is all ours, Madame. What brings you so far from Sherburne?

AIMEE. Obedience to your nephew, Colonel. Good evening, Nicholas.

NICHOLAS. Good evening, Marquise. Pray tell us in which particular you obeyed poor Nicholas.

AIMEE. Well, it was you who bade me look at the sunset from the eastern part of the island. What do you call it?

STARBUCK. 'Sconset, Marquise?

AIMEE. No, we drove a little beyond —

STARBUCK. Ah, to Sancoty Head it was.

AIMEE. That's it.

NICHOLAS. You weren't disappointed, I hope.

AIMEE. Most certainly not. Sunsets are my passion — and this one took me back to my childhood. My family, the Fapignac, owned a small property on the Breton coast where the sunsets resembled yours. The rugged land, you know, the wild sea, the steeples. I was enchanted.

STARBUCK. It is a romantic evening, is it not?

AIMEE. Yes. And now this splendid moon! But you gentlemen — I seem to have stumbled upon a band of conspirators! I find you miles from Sherburne —

NICHOLAS. A mere three miles, Madame.

AIMEE. It seems farther because of the wildness. I am quite sure I have found you out in some wickedness. How delightful. Your men are staring at me.

NICHOLAS. They are amazed to see this fairy-tale apparition by a fisherman's hut.

AIMEE. Who knows what is concealed in that hut? I am determined to enjoy something extraordinary and positively forbidden.

STARBUCK. Where is your charming daughter, Marquise?

AIMEE. No, you cannot fob me off, Colonel. There's mischief in the air. Would that it were directed against our enemy! So speaks a Frenchwoman.

NICHOLAS. It grieves me to —

STARBUCK. No, no, Madame has discovered us, Nick; I think we had better confess.

(*NICHOLAS stares at him*)

OBED. Colonel —

STARBUCK. But do you swear not to give us away, Marquise?

AIMEE. I swear! This is wonderfully exciting.

STARBUCK. Still, I tremble. Can we repose our trust in your word, Marquise?

AIMEE. I swear on the bones of Bertrand de Fapignac, the founder of our house. Does that satisfy you?

STARBUCK. It must. Well then — we are — you shan't forget your oath, Madame?

AIMEE. I swear again.

STARBUCK. You are irresistible. I am afraid you surprised us bargaining for ten barrels of rum to be delivered on this spot a week from today. But you'll give us away, Marquise.

AIMEE. Trust me, Colonel. However, your ten barrels of rum are a disappointment. What barrels? Where from? And why this nighttime huddle?

STARBUCK. These barrels — as a man of honor I detest the word, Marquise, but they are being *smuggled* into the island.

NICHOLAS. Dreadful times.

OBED. Terrible times.

STARBUCK. I am deeply embarrassed at being found out a common smuggler.

AIMEE. Nonsense — my grandfather on my mother's side, the Comte d'Epervisse, took smuggled tobacco all his life. But why are you smuggling rum? Isn't your rum distilled, or whatever you do with rum, here in your own Massachusetts?

STARBUCK. We have it from Rhode Island, Madame. We are landing it secretly — but I shouldn't tell you, for you are a friend of Captain Cuff's.

AIMEE. That bulldog? You know better, Colonel.

STARBUCK. Then I can speak freely. Captain Cuff would seize the rum and ship it to General Gage at Boston. Now we are peace-loving and law-abiding citizens, we hate rebellion, but is it our duty to drink water for King George? We say, let Boston find its own rum. Besides, the loss of their customary supply would cause our people to grumble against the king.

AIMEE. Enjoy your rum, Colonel. You didn't leave *all* my romantic needs unsatisfied — though I was hoping for something — oh I don't know — a trifle more dashing — a plot to seize Captain Cuff — to smuggle in a cannon or two — to make an escape from the island — who knows?

NICHOLAS. Only rebels would do such naughty things. No, Marquise, this is a prosaic island. Nothing but whales and cod.

AIMEE. And a few sheep, mules and asses grazing in the fields.

NICHOLAS. There you have it.

AIMEE. Well, it's getting to be a chilly night, and Madeleine will fidget if I don't return presently. Good evening, gentlemen, and happily met.

STARBUCK and NICHOLAS. Good evening, Marquise.

STARBUCK. Bid old Moses look out for the ruts on your way home.

AIMEE. Thank you. I will.

(*She leaves*)

NICHOLAS (*low and quickly*). She's a dangerous gossip. She'll go straight to Cuff or Weamish. Damn it, we must prevent her. Marquise!

STARBUCK. What are you doing?

VOICE OF AIMEE. Did you call me?

NICHOLAS. Yes — wait for me, Marquise! (*To STARBUCK*) I'll escort her to Swain's — put Wallis and rum together — leave it to me.

STARBUCK. But don't overdo it.

NICHOLAS (*leaving*). Marquise, I can't allow you to drive alone in this darkness. Old Moses, bless him, is half blind. You didn't notice? Allow me —

MAMACK. I try to keep my face hidden.

STARBUCK. I know. That was a mistake, Mamack. It made us look more suspicious.

OBED. You're quite the story-teller, Colonel.

STARBUCK. Thank you. I believe the lady would ruin a kingdom if the privilege of spreading the news was hers. Come home with me, Obed. Mamack, better if you go back your own way.

MAMACK. I hope I didn't spoil nothing.

STARBUCK. I'm sure you didn't. (*He puts his arm around MAMACK's shoulders*) Run along now.

MAMACK. Thank you, Colonel. You know where to find me. Good night, Mr. Coffin.

OBED. Good night, Josh.

(*MAMACK leaves*)

STARBUCK. You and I will wait up at the home till young Nick rejoins us. If the Marquise is safe in bed, we'll march to the Judge's house, raise a storm over Wallis, and make up a tale about our presence here that will forestall any gossip of hers. And now I think of it, I promised the Captain to look for secret stores of ammunition. This then was our employment tonight. It will bolster our demand that Wallis be set free.

OBED. We'll break the jail down if need be, Colonel.

STARBUCK. Gad, my nephew was right. We'll have much to be thankful for on Sunday — if we live to see it.

SCENE EIGHT

(*Friday, June 23. One o'clock in the morning. Second story of Swain's Tavern. AIMEE's bedroom. We also see a portion of the landing, and a couple of doors leading to other rooms. The bed is of the alcove type, surrounded by curtains.*

NICHOLAS is putting on his clothes)

NICHOLAS. You're not falling asleep, Amy?

AIMEE'S VOICE (*from the bed*). Aimée, you puppy, Aimée. I insist.

NICHOLAS. Not while you're in my country, and never again for me. Not for me, d'you hear?

AIMEE. Yes for you. And you, sir, are Nicolas — Nee-ko-lah (*she pronounces the name in French*) when we're alone. Not Nick, young Nick, Nicky, or any other vulgar middle-class nick-names. (*They both laugh*) Give me another kiss, you villain, you seducer of elderly ladies.

NICHOLAS. No, Marquise.

AIMEE. Why not?

NICHOLAS. Twenty kisses or nothing.

AIMEE. So be it. Twenty kisses.

(*NICHOLAS flings himself onto the bed and vanishes from sight*)

AIMEE. Not so hard, darling.

NICHOLAS. Witch — mermaid — sorceress — so much pleasure no man ever tasted before — and survived to remember it.

AIMEE. The pleasure was mine, sir.

NICHOLAS. No, no, it couldn't — it wasn't —

AIMEE. It will improve with time, and is keen already. My pretty boy. What thrilling eyelashes you have, and what sweet silky lips. Mmmmm. Ah if I were twenty years younger!

NICHOLAS. I refuse to listen! You are a masterpiece of nature. Don't grow a day younger or I shall cut my throat. Let us enjoy, enjoy, enjoy. Ah I wish I could, once more — if I stayed till dawn —

AIMEE. What are you thinking of? Silly Yankee! There will be other times, I hope — or will you toss me aside, like the rind of an orange you've devoured?

NICHOLAS. You are my inexhaustible orange tree! Permit me, Marquise, to nibble again.

AIMEE. Pray do. Mmmmm. A little more . . .

NICHOLAS. Your loyal servant . . .

AIMEE. Ah!

NICHOLAS. Pleased?

AIMEE. Delighted.

NICHOLAS. I must be gone, mustn't I? Come by the window with me. Let us have a tiny conversation before you send me away.

AIMEE (lazily). Very well.

(They reappear)

NICHOLAS. May I? (He helps her with a scanty robe) Oh how yielding and warm you feel through this gauze!

AIMEE. I thought we were going to converse?

NICHOLAS. By all means. (They sit on an upholstered bench by the window) You're not chilly?

AIMEE. I will be if you take your arm away.

NICHOLAS. Amy — what next? Tell me.

AIMEE. Anything you wish, my darling rebel.

NICHOLAS. Rebel? Who is a rebel?

AIMEE. My daughter's suitor.

NICHOLAS (startled). Madeleine told you?

AIMEE. She made such a serious point of not telling me that I understood at once.

NICHOLAS. You must think me an infinite scoundrel.

AIMEE. That's why I love you, my daredevil.

NICHOLAS. Are you a daredevil too?

AIMEE. In a modest way.

NICHOLAS. Do you dare — marry me?

AIMEE. Even though I am her mother?

NICHOLAS. I was a fool. It seemed romantic. But it was too pale, too prim, too strait-laced. It would have been a disaster after a month. You, instead — you shall dance with me through life.

AIMEE. And yet, there on the beach, were you not setting out to dance across the water without me?

NICHOLAS. Amy! What has Madeleine told you about us?

AIMEE. She tells her mother very little. But when I saw you tonight huddled together, I suddenly knew it all. I teased you because I was so glad.

NICHOLAS. What a relief for me! Now I needn't preach the good cause before you marry me.

AIMEE. Did I say I'll marry you, sir?

NICHOLAS. Do, my love, do. I'll devote my life to turning your regrets into as many gratitudes. I'll not buckle my shoe without consulting your happiness. What say you, Amy?

AIMEE. Let me taste again. (*She kisses him*) Yes . . . I'd be sorry to lose this. But my name, Nicolas, my name. I know your family is respectable — very fair for America. And you are a man of some means —

NICHOLAS. More than some, Amy; listen to me. I have a privateering commission in my pocket, commitments for a fleet out of Salem, the guarantee of a prodigious —

AIMEE (*stopping her ears*). Ta ta ta ta! Spare me these horrors! I hope you'll not oblige me to do your arithmetic for you. No. My question is, how can I parade you — setting aside the difference in age —

NICHOLAS. Amy, does Venus obey a calendar? Your skin is all cream and roses —

AIMEE. But how can I present you to Monsieur — to the King — or for that matter to my uncle, the Baron d'Alberny?

NICHOLAS. Amy, *my* uncle has been named brigadier in the new army. We've received extraordinary orders to report to Cambridge. I scorn to boast —

AIMEE. Because your soul is noble, and that is the only nobility of any consequence to me. But the world!

NICHOLAS. God! You'll drive me to distraction! Shall I leave at once?

AIMEE. No!

NICHOLAS. Why return to France at all? I mean to be a king myself, in Virginia or in the Carolines. You and I will hold court in a plantation. You'll walk on my arm as my consort. And when we Americans come to make titles of our own — need I say more? Forget your musty, doddering France. This is the new world, the new life — trust your passionate buccaneer —

AIMEE. Tempter! Your words intoxicate me — hold me close to you — I'll do anything you ask. I know! I'll renounce my title for your sake.

NICHOLAS. Oh no!

AIMEE. Then take me as I am.

NICHOLAS. Amy, Amy, my wife! (*They kiss*) Who would have thought, when I ran after you — ?

AIMEE. Why *did* you run after me, you rascal?

NICHOLAS. You gave us such a start when you happened upon our meeting.

AIMEE. I know I did, but why? Surely Madeleine had told you I was your friend from the beginning.

NICHOLAS. Oh yes, and yet we fancied that you might be tattling to the Judge over a cup of chocolate, in all innocence of course. I decided to escort you, plead for discretion, and — to tell you the truth — seduce you if necessary.

AIMEE. And I — to tell you the truth — decided to let you.

NICHOLAS. Oh the hussy!

AIMEE. Oh the scamp!

(*They kiss*)

NICHOLAS. Shall we go back — there (*he points to the bed*) — or make projects for our lives?

AIMEE. My wifely voice says, we had better make projects for our lives.

NICHOLAS. And begin soberly with the beginning. We were struck a nasty blow earlier this evening, Amy. I had resolved to confide in you on our way here, but — certain interruptions came between me and my story.

AIMEE. What story, my pretty lad?

NICHOLAS. About the steward, the so-called steward who almost drowned.

AIMEE. Why so-called?

NICHOLAS. I'm afraid we saw no way but to pretend. He was in fact our agent, Henry Wallis by name.

AIMEE. The tricks you men play!

NICHOLAS. They don't always suffice. Several townspeople recognized him, and Captain Cuff arrested him tonight.

(*AIMEE jumps up. Her tone is very different now*)

AIMEE. While I was — ! Hang the ruffian!

NICHOLAS. If Wallis confesses that he came ashore to plot our escape from Nantucket, we'll be in jail with him tomorrow.

AIMEE. We must fight this Captain, Nicholas.

NICHOLAS. We will, darling. What a comfort to see you so indignant! We'll not go flower-picking while they confirm their suspicions. My plan's already formed. My uncle, myself and ten armed men will overcome our booby of a Judge, use him for a hostage, and force our way to my uncle's sloop. Wallis must fend for himself, as he was fool enough to be caught. And you and Madeleine will join us at Cambridge in your own good time.

AIMEE. No, no, no. I hate your scheme. You underestimate the captain, Nicholas. Ten men indeed! He has ten times that number of trained soldiers.

NICHOLAS. And we have most of Sherburne!

AIMEE. Worse still! You're too young, you believe you're indestructible! But I know better; I've seen too many indestructible youngsters bleeding to death in the snow! Leave it all to me instead.

NICHOLAS. To you!

AIMEE. Ah — I see you still mistrust me.

NICHOLAS. No, Amy — but how — what in the world can you do?

AIMEE. I can denounce you.

NICHOLAS. What do you mean?

AIMEE. I'll play the spy. I'll inform against you. You'll see. To save you I'll become clever. I'll stop that bully of a Captain. Tomorrow — I mean later today — I'll send out dinner invitations to you, your uncle, the Captain, and the Judge. I'll serve them an unforgettable meal, I promise you. Before dessert is on the table, your enemies will be in your hands, bound and gagged; you shall walk to your beach in triumph. And meet me there.

NICHOLAS. You leave me speechless! Is this my tender Marquise?

AIMEE. I know — you thought me nothing but a gossip, a dainty mistress for a night —

NICHOLAS. Amy!

AIMEE. Instead I'll show you a tigress.

NICHOLAS. More and more marvelous! But what will you prepare for these gentlemen? A sleeping potion? A brew to make them mad? A Borgia poison?

AIMEE. Tat, tat, curiosity killed the cat. Hurry to your uncle now. He must think you're in jail.

NICHOLAS. By God, you're right. But when shall I hear the rest?

AIMEE. Before noon. And kiss me before you go.

NICHOLAS. Must I leave you?

AIMEE. I wish I could say no. But you must. Wait, I'll see you out.

(*AIMEE lights a taper and they walk out together. On the landing they embrace again. One of the doors opens, and MADELEINE appears in her nightdress, also holding a taper*)

AIMEE. Madeleine! What are you doing here stark naked?

MADELEINE. Why, I'm as decorously dressed as you, mamma.

NICHOLAS. My dear Madeleine, embarrassment is useless, concealment impossible: I am your new father. I aspired at one time to another, more intimate connection — but you gave me my freedom, which I hastened to surrender to this precious lady, your mother, who is, indeed, more precious to me for being your mother.

MADELEINE. My dear new father, and mother dear, I offer you my tenderest congratulations. Be assured of all the obedience due from a virtuous daughter. But permit me to withdraw at this time.

NICHOLAS. By no means! I am the intruder here, the thief in the night who has snatched away a priceless pearl. (*He kisses AIMEE's hand*) I wish you a restful night, though little remains of it. My dearest Marquise, will you convey all the necessary intelligence to our Madeleine?

AIMEE. I will, my angel.

NICHOLAS. Good night, then. (*To MADELEINE*) Good night, my dear.

AIMEE. Good night.

(*NICHOLAS goes down the stairs and disappears. The two women stand without speaking until they hear the door downstairs close behind NICHOLAS*)

AIMEE (*very excited*). Come with me, Madeleine. (*She takes MADELEINE by the hand back into her room*) Put down your candle. Madelon! We're changing sides!

MADELEINE. I thought as much from the noises I heard.

AIMEE. Isn't it exciting? All my political opinions are turned upside down. I'm as hot a revolutionary now as you are, you baggage. And I'm going to commit a ghastly misalliance by marrying Nicholas Starbuck.

MADELEINE. What will the Baron d'Alberny say when he gets wind of this tragic degradation?

AIMEE. Ah, I'm so glad you're taking it lightly. I was terrified — I thought you'd make a great moral scene on the landing. Madelon, my little canary, you're not jealous of your old mother, are you? I didn't take him away from you — you practically bequeathed him to me.

MADELEINE. I don't want to bequeath him to you, mother, because of what will happen when he learns the truth.

AIMEE. Why should he learn anything so unpleasant?

MADELEINE. Because your former friends will see to it.

AIMEE. No, my girl. I know too many of their secrets. However, I'll secure myself on Nicholas' side as well. You'll see.

MADELEINE. I don't think I'll see. I'll go back to Lyon.

AIMEE. What do you mean, "back"? You're a stranger in France.

MADELEINE. What of it? Tante Marie has asked me often enough; she has a small room for me; and I'll help her mind the shop.

AIMEE. You've always wanted fire. You're destined to marry a tailor — and be faithful to him.

MADELEINE. I'm sorry I've disappointed you, mother.

AIMEE. Nonsense. Come here. (*She kisses her*)

MADELEINE. Where next, mamma? Do we leave the island with the Starbucks?

AIMEE. It's not so easy as that. The Captain has arrested their agent — the very man my young hero rescued from the ocean the other day.

MADELEINE. I see.

AIMEE. If he gives evidence, our Starbucks are lost, so is my credit, I'm widowed for the third time, and then I may as well return to Lyon to keep shop with you. But we're not there yet. Not while I'm playing cards on both sides of the table.

MADELEINE. What do you propose to do?

AIMEE. I propose to give a dinner for the two parties, and serve one party as a main course for the other.

MADELEINE. Someone might be killed, in other words.

AIMEE. If anyone is killed, he'll have only himself to blame. I'll give the blackguards every chance to surrender meekly.

MADELEINE. And what do you expect *me* to do?

AIMEE. You? I expect you to show me all the obedience due from a virtuous daughter. You kept your wits about you, I must say.

MADELEINE. Mother, mother! How much longer shall we live by these odious schemes?

AIMEE. This will be our last, Madelon; one more — and then — God help me — I'll miss them.

SCENE NINE

(Friday, June 23. Morning. The WEAMISH residence. WEAMISH is finishing another letter)

WEAMISH. "Therefore hasten your return, dearest mamma; the kingdom's fate is being decided here; all is lost without you. Your devoted and beleaguered son — " Jenny!
(Instead of JENNY, AIMEE enters)
AIMEE. Urgent matters, Judge; I could not wait to be announced.
WEAMISH. Welcome, welcome, Marquise! The world is crumbling. The fate of our kingdom is being decided here. Captain Cuff has arrested a man who proves to be a secret emissary for the Starbucks. The population is up in arms. I tremble for my life. The Starbucks stormed and fumed where you are standing now ere I had set my lips to my morning coffee. Anarchy is let loose upon the land, and I predict the Last Judgment is not far off.
AIMEE. Control yourself, Judge; I am here to help you. The news of Henry Wallis' unauthorized arrest reached me a few minutes after it happened.
WEAMISH. Oh, what comfort you bring me, Madame. You even know his name.
AIMEE. You may recollect that I became suspicious at once when the man was rescued, and made strenuous attempts to have our mulish Captain convey the fellow to our own quarters. Captain Cuff understands only blunderbusses and twenty-pounders.
WEAMISH. Thank God for your presence here, Marquise. With you at my side, I shall smite to the left and right of me. I shall spare no one.
(Enter JENNY)
JENNY. It's Captain Cuff to see you.
WEAMISH. Have him come up at once. And take this *(he is about to offer the letter)* — no, it can wait.
JENNY. Yes, sir.
(She leaves as Captain Cuff enters)

CUFF. Good morning all.

AIMEE. Good —

CUFF. Y'are here to give me a dressing down by leave of General Gage. Consider it done. I arrested that rascal of an agent on my own initiative.

WEAMISH. Let me inform you, Captain, that the Starbucks burst into this room at dawn and vented their rage upon my person.

CUFF. Let them vent upon mine. I'll teach 'em to rage, the scurvy rebels.

WEAMISH. You call them rebels. But does Mr. Wallis confess he came here on a political mission?

CUFF. He hasn't confessed yet, but leave him to me until Sunday, and after church I'll serve you a confession on a platter.

AIMEE. By Sunday the Starbucks will be in Cambridge.

WEAMISH and CUFF. What?

AIMEE. I repeat: By Sunday the two Starbucks will be in Cambridge. Wallis came here to take them off the island. The rendez-vous will take place without him. (*Imitating the captain*) Y'are too slow, Captain Cuff.

CUFF. Od's guts, who told you all this?

WEAMISH. Marquise — ?

AIMEE. I never reveal the sources of my intelligence, gentlemen. But I hope you credit me. If you do not, the event will speak for me soon enough.

CUFF. Od's guts, who told you all this?

AIMEE. I never reveal the sources of my intelligence, gentlemen. But I hope you credit me. If you do not, the event will speak for me soon enough.

CUFF. I credit you so thoroughly that I'm off to arrest them both. I should have done it the day you arrived. It was you that kept me. Od's liver, I smell a vile rebel a league away. Judge, write me out a warrant. We'll do it by the book this time.

WEAMISH. Sign a warrant against the Starbucks? Who settled here in 1659? I'll be stoned to death.

AIMEE. Judge Weamish is right. He is interested in avoiding bloodshed.

CUFF. I'm not.

AIMEE. To each his profession. But a soldier's first duty, as I understand —

CUFF. Is to destroy the enemy.

AIMEE. Is not to be destroyed by the enemy. That's a *sine qua non* for the other.

CUFF. The devil of a sinecure it is! Madam, with all due —

AIMEE. Captain, with all due, arresting the Starbucks in the open is not advisable. Twenty-five to thirty armed patriots are standing guard over their house; others are milling about your quarters; more are gathering in the street below.

WEAMISH. Merciful gods!

AIMEE. Your life is not safe, Judge; and yours even less, Captain. Granted, these yokels are untrained, but they come in large crowds, they shoot in all directions, and they are philosophical enough to hide behind fences and trees. Must a woman teach you these nursery-school facts?

WEAMISH. I am taught, Marquise; consider me your devoted pupil.

AIMEE. Captain?

CUFF. The women are in command here. I see we must go by ruses and devices.

AIMEE. Be patient, Captain. I am reserving a capital role for brawn and firepower. Will you both kindly dine with me tomorrow in Mr. Swain's private dining room? Shall we say at one in the afternoon? This will be a modest repayment for the many delicate attentions I have received at Sherburne since my arrival.

WEAMISH. This is handsome, Madame. But what of the entertainment I had designed?

AIMEE. Another time. May I count on your company, my dear Judge? (WEAMISH kisses her hand) And yours, Captain?

CUFF (fuming). Hang good manners, this flummery has gone too far!

AIMEE. My other guests will be Colonel and Mr. Starbuck.

(Effect)

CUFF. I'll be there.

WEAMISH. I don't know, Marquise, whether —

AIMEE. Perfectly within the bounds of decorum, Judge. As a French neutral, I wish to bring the two sides in the Wallis affair together for explanation, negotiation, and conciliation. I suggest, Captain, that you also invite two of your trusted men, and place them within earshot in the cellar. When the meat is served, the Judge will propose a toast to His Majesty. The moment the glasses are raised, you, my dear Captain, will produce a pistol in the intimacy of our dining room and summon your two warriors.

CUFF. Marquise, I apologize for my sour words.

AIMEE. I have forgotten them.

WEAMISH (pale). What if —

AIMEE. Yes?

WEAMISH. What if the Starbucks are armed?

CUFF. I hope they are. We'll cut 'em down on the spot. It will save Tom Gage a trial.

WEAMISH. Shoot them? At the table? Before two ladies?

CUFF. Before or behind. It's all the same to me.

AIMEE. I hope they will have enough breeding to offer no resistance. The fact is, they will be disarmed before we sit down to dinner.

CUFF. How will you manage that?

AIMEE. Easily. Give me your pistol, Captain. Yes, your weapon. Thank you. I shall place it on a footstool under the table and cover it with a cushion. At your entrance, you'll offer to be searched, and demand to do likewise upon the Starbucks. Are you right-handed? I shall sit to your right, and at the critical moment I shall give you the weapon.

WEAMISH. What if the Starbucks will not dine without their firearms?

AIMEE. Our nakedness will lull them all the same, and Captain Cuff will be prompt enough to amaze them as soon as I hand him the pistol.

CUFF. I'll amaze them out of a year's growth, I will.

WEAMISH. Permit me, Marquise. Why not try gentler means?

CUFF. With a man like Nicholas Starbuck?

WEAMISH. The Starbucks are all persons of birth and consequence, Captain; they are not Trinidad pirates.

AIMEE. What is your proposal, Judge?

WEAMISH. Suppose that when the fruit is brought in after dinner, I turn to the Colonel, and inform him with my severest demeanor that important disclosures have come to my attention. "Colonel Starbuck," I shall say, "unimpeachable revelations have reached my ears; discoveries of the gravest character, conveyed by private informants whom, needless to say, I am not at liberty to name — "

CUFF. By the time y'are done with that fine Oxford sentence, the rascals will have cut our throats.

WEAMISH. No, Captain, I believe they will be mute. But to oblige you I shall be more direct. "In short," I shall say, "I know that you and your lively nephew are harboring a secret purpose, injurious to the peace of this nation and contrary to that cheerful subordination which has hitherto made the happiness of these colonies — an attempt, I am told, to escape from Nantucket with the object of joining —

CUFF. Et caetera, et caetera, et caetera.

WEAMISH. Just so. "But now," I shall continue, "your avenues are barred. Captain Cuff has surrounded these premises" — and to be sure, Captain, have Sergeant O'Toole lead a detachment to the tavern. With this terrifying news I shall rise to my feet — no, I believe I am on my feet already — and call upon the Starbucks to renounce their wicked purpose. "As you hope for eternal salvation of your souls in the world hereafter, and ease, honor, and comfort in your present existence, you now solemnly swear that you shall cease to be the treacherous ministers of satanic rebellion, and that you shall uphold his Majesty George III, defend the British Constitution, and lend the support of your arms to his Majesty's forces."

CUFF. Ha, ha, ha, ha!

WEAMISH. Why are you laughing, Captain?

CUFF. Because my bedtime will have come before y'ave run through that monstrous oath!

WEAMISH. I —

CUFF. No, Judge, excuse me. I'm a raw fellow, I know, I ran from school when I was nine, but this will never do. If we let the Starbucks slip out of our hands tomorrow, we deserve to be hanged without benefit of clergy.

AIMEE. Your plan has distinct merit, Judge; but what if the Starbucks, besides refusing to dine unarmed, bring along a detachment of their own? I foresee a general massacre.

WEAMISH. Oh.

AIMEE. My own contrivance seems a little less boisterous, on the whole.

CUFF. If y'are afraid for your life, Judge, you can *pretend* to faint the moment I aim my pistol at the Starbucks.

WEAMISH. I am not afraid for my life, Captain, though I know full well — and better than you, if I may say so — that to deprive Nantucket of its royal magistrate at this juncture would be to invite mere chaos. But I bow to the majority. Have it your way. You'll not see me flinch.

CUFF. That's settled then. We tie up our two Starbucks and deliver them to the jailhouse.

AIMEE. No, Captain. Remember the confederates outside. Mr. Swain shall let it be known that the negotiations are continuing through the night, and when all are dispersed, we shall secrete our prisoners to the harbor and ship them at once to Boston.

WEAMISH. What if they decline your invitation in the first place, Marquise? Have you thought of that?

AIMEE. They cannot decline. They must keep up the pretense that Wallis is their business agent, and they are mortally afraid that if he is not released, he'll betray them.

WEAMISH. If you say so.

CUFF. Well, that concludes our palaver. I'll see to my side of the plan; the men to be posted in the cellar —

AIMEE. No more than two — one might suffice.

CUFF. No, we'll stick to two. They'll bring a couple of halyards along to tie up our rebels. If we're obliged to open fire, let the ladies dive under the table and you, Judge, pacify the rabble that's sure to come running. Are you staying, Marquise?

AIMEE. No, Captain, I'm coming with you. Don't forget the toast, Judge; loud and clear, so the soldiers can hear you — our lives may depend on it.

WEAMISH. Yes, Marquise.

AIMEE. Till tomorrow, then. At one.

WEAMISH. Yes, Marquise.

CUFF. Good day, Judge.

WEAMISH. Good day, Captain.

(*AIMEE and CUFF leave*)

WEAMISH (*alone*). Death and damnation! Why did I allow these firebrands to overrule me? I'm the chief magistrate, by all that's holy! He'll amaze them, will he? Suppose they decline to be amazed and shoot? And that infernal Frenchwoman! I've learned my lesson for the future: stay away from foreigners, Tom Weamish! Future? What future? Oh mother, do you see me sprawled on Mr. Swain's floor with a bullet through my heart? That peasant of a Captain has little enough to live for, but I'm in line for a seat in the Council, confound it! What business has a man like me to meddle with a vulgar ambush? Let the ruffians fight it out among themselves. I'm no such fool after all. I shall have Jenny call me home after the soup to settle some dispute. Let Mistress Spy pledge the King in my place. Loud and clear, so the soldiers in the cellar can run to her rescue. Let them all amaze one another, while I — Jenny! Jenny!

JENNY'S VOICE. Yes, sir?

WEAMISH. Come here! I must give you particular commands!

JENNY'S VOICE. I can't. I'm busy folding linen in the kitchen.

WEAMISH (*furious*). Damn the kitchen! Come up at once, or I'll bloody your face! (*To himself*) Pshaw! I'm a wild beast when I'm crossed.

SCENE TEN

(*Friday, June 23. Afternoon. The same lane and bench as in Scene Five. This time ELIAS STARBUCK is sitting and reading a book, and MADELEINE approaches, halts, and looks at him. Signs of inward struggle in her face. STARBUCK senses her presence and turns around*)

STARBUCK. Oh, Mademoiselle de Tourville! Good afternoon.

MADELEINE. Good afternoon . . .

STARBUCK. Are you hurrying somewhere?

MADELEINE. No.

STARBUCK. I'm so glad. May I make a confession?

MADELEINE. A confession?

STARBUCK. I was hoping to meet you here — and to have you share the sunshine with me for half an hour.

MADELEINE. Gladly.

(*She sits down next to him*)

MADELEINE. Are you still reading Mr. Stevenson's book?

STARBUCK. Mr. Jefferson's pamphlet?

MADELEINE. Yes.

STARBUCK. I finished it somehow between one urgent matter and another. I believe I would get to the end of a book even though I were called into battle and obliged to read on horseback. I have no peace until I conclude.

MADELEINE. This new one is slender enough to finish by tomorrow, I suppose.

STARBUCK. Yes — by tomorrow.

MADELEINE. May I ask what it is?

STARBUCK. If you do not, I shall tell you without being asked, for I took it down from my shelf thinking of you. (*He gives her the little book*)

MADELEINE. "Elihu Coleman, of Nantucket. 'A Testimony Against That Anti-Christian Practice of MAKING SLAVES OF MEN.' " In very large letters!

STARBUCK. The date is here.

MADELEINE. 1729.

STARBUCK. Aye; I was eight years old then; but I remember Mr. Coleman. He was a Quaker minister, and, for this modest island of ours, a learned man. We Starbucks prayed in the Episcopal church — still do, of course. We felt something of a superiority over these prim Quakers. But now I am proud of old Mr. Coleman. Few men before him, if any, had spoken out against slavery. All Christianity was content to emulate the pagans in their vilest practice. But not old Mr. Coleman of Nantucket, bless him.

MADELEINE. This is pretty: "Now although the Turks make slaves of those they catch that are not of their religion, yet (as history relates) as soon as any embraces the Mahometan religion, they are no longer kept slaves, but are quickly set free, and for the most part put to some place of preferment; so zealous are they for proselytes and their own religion. Now if many among those called Christians would but consider, how far they fall short of the Turks in this particular, it would be well; for they tell the Negroes, that they must believe in Christ, and receive the Christian faith, and that they must receive the sacrament, and be baptized, and so they do; but still they keep them slaves for all this."

STARBUCK. Yes — it is pretty, as you say. Mr. Coleman does not stray far beyond the obvious, but far beyond the obvious is often an artificial and a useless place. Read; let me not interrupt you.

(There is a silence, while MADELEINE reads a little. Then she returns the book to STARBUCK)

MADELEINE (softly). You will struggle to make this America of yours stainless?

STARBUCK. Without oppressors and without victims at any rate.

MADELEINE. Can this ever be?

STARBUCK. I must believe it. My own happiness will be hobbled as long as I know that somewhere black men are being abused, Indians robbed, other white men persecuted. Oh, this reminds me. Look, here is an old Indian stone pipe. It's one of a very few left on the island.

MADELEINE. It has such a contented look! Is it very old?

STARBUCK. Perhaps a century; perhaps more. They smoked these long before we Englishmen came. An Indian told me they used a weed they called poke. It no longer grows here.

MADELEINE. I want to puff on it!

STARBUCK. Please do. (They both laugh) It's not really a stone pipe, you know, though they call it that. It's made of a mixture of blue clay and mussel shells, pounded, mixed, and burnt.

MADELEINE. Thank you for showing it to me.

STARBUCK. May I leave it for you at Swain's, to remember us?

(There is a silence)

MADELEINE. I'll never part with it. (Another pause) Have you heard — what has taken place — between your nephew — and —

STARBUCK. Yes, I've heard. We are going to be relations!

MADELEINE. Yes.

STARBUCK. Does it disturb you very much that — I mean — the difference in their age —

MADELEINE. Not at all. Not that. And you?

STARBUCK. Then it's something else. I am afraid you feel the insult to your name —

MADELEINE. Oh God, never say such a thing again! Never never —

STARBUCK. What is it, then? Are you in love with him after all?

MADELEINE. Oh no —

STARBUCK. Why shouldn't you be? He has so much —

MADELEINE. I am not — I really am not. I ask you to believe me!

STARBUCK. I will. But then — of course! I am a proper fool! You are wondering what's to become of you — you don't know where to turn —

MADELEINE. No, no. Everything is decently arranged. I have an aunt in France who has often begged me to come. I will see my country for the first time.

STARBUCK. True; you have never been in France.

MADELEINE. I was a baby when we left.

STARBUCK. How far away . . . But surely you will return one day to your mother — holding court, no doubt, wherever young Nick decides to fix. She is, I must confess, a *grande dame* such as we have never seen in these parts. You and I shall visit the happy couple together.

MADELEINE. I will never see her again.

STARBUCK. You do feel the disgrace after all.

MADELEINE (*getting up*). Again! I must go —

STARBUCK. Wait! And forgive me. I ought to know you better. Don't go before I make a request of you. (*He takes her hand and pulls her down again*) It's a matter of extreme importance.

MADELEINE. Anything.

STARBUCK. We have said nothing about tomorrow's dinner.

MADELEINE. The less said, the better.

STARBUCK. Madeleine: I demand that you stay away. *Demand* it.

MADELEINE. My mother —

STARBUCK (*suddenly angry, standing up*). I don't care! I intend to tell the Marquise that if you appear at table, I will quit the game at once, happen what may.

MADELEINE. But if I promise you I shan't spoil anything? I have as much courage —

STARBUCK. What do you mean? Who said you were going to spoil anything?

MADELEINE. Then why shouldn't I be present?

STARBUCK. How can you ask? No, you can't possibly misunderstand me! (*MADELEINE looks long into his eyes*) Do you promise me, Madeleine? Do I have your solemn promise?

MADELEINE (*almost inaudibly*). I promise you.

(*She leaves slowly, her head bowed. STARBUCK remains alone. He watches her for a while, then pensively sits down again. He fingers through his book and tries to read)*

STARBUCK. "Now I would have all to consider . . . " *(he pauses, dreams, resumes)* "of this practice of making slaves of Negroes, to see what the original of it was, whether pride and idleness was not the first rise of it," *(same interruption; he looks where MADELEINE went)* "that they might go with white hands, and that their wives might, like Jezebel, paint and adorn themselves . . . " *(He stops, and grows pensive again)*

(Reenter MADELEINE. She sits down without a word, while STARBUCK looks at her in anxious surprise)

MADELEINE *(low)*. My name is Madeleine Pichot.

(Pause)

STARBUCK. Pichot? Pichot de Tourville?

MADELEINE *(she is forced to smile)*. No. Plain Pichot. It's a name that makes people laugh in my country.

STARBUCK. Then you are not the Marquise's daughter?

MADELEINE. Indeed I am.

STARBUCK. Ah!

MADELEINE. Her name is Aimée Pichot. We are both in the pay of General Gage. Vulgar spies. Mother and daughter. Our destination is Canada, but we paused here for an important special mission, namely to discover whether you are rebels, and to have you arrested if you are.

STARBUCK. That is to say, tomorrow, at table?

MADELEINE. No. My mother has changed sides. Madame de Tourville intends to become the noble wife of an immensely rich Yankee.

STARBUCK. And you?

MADELEINE. I do have an aunt in Lyon. She is a milliner. The hat shop will be *my* plantation.

STARBUCK. Tell me, Madeleine. Have you yourself been a spy? In Canada? In New York? Here? Not you.

MADELEINE *(low)*. I never ran away.

STARBUCK. Is your father living?

MADELEINE. I don't know.

STARBUCK. How is that?

MADELEINE. Because I don't know who he is, and neither does my mother. She was married once to a turnkey in Lyon; but he was not my father. When he died, a nobleman took her for his mistress; but he was not my father either. My father may be the baron's bailiff whose name she has forgotten, or one of his footmen or dog-keepers, or else the sergeant who once struck the baron's face and eventually ran off with mother to Canada. I was two years old when he died. My mother has also been —

STARBUCK. Tell me, don't be afraid.

MADELEINE. Gage's mistress.

STARBUCK. And you?

MADELEINE. Why should you believe anything I say about myself?

STARBUCK *(softly)*. Let *me* decide.

MADELEINE. There was a boy in New York — it was quickly over —

STARBUCK. And now — have you "changed sides" too?

MADELEINE. No.

STARBUCK (smiling). Do you mean you're still a stubborn Tory?

MADELEINE. I never was.

(A pause)

STARBUCK. Do you hate her, Madeleine?

MADELEINE. My mother? I have been a dead weight for her to carry, and yet she brought me up, gave me teachers, groomed me to be a lady, and now — I betray her. But done is done. Someone was bound to be betrayed. You or she. Now the knowledge is yours to use.

STARBUCK. What would you have me do with it?

MADELEINE. Why do you ask me?

STARBUCK. I simply choose to.

(A pause)

MADELEINE. Say nothing until the Judge and the Captain are in your hands. Then tell your nephew the truth, and go.

STARBUCK. And leave you on the island with your mother? Do you understand that she will be shot by the British?

MADELEINE (frightened). Then take her with you! She's risking her life for you tomorrow! She'll do you no harm — !

STARBUCK. Calm yourself. She'll sail with us. No one will injure her. But that leaves yourself.

MADELEINE. I have enough for the journey to France. Will you let me go? Think of this. I must live in my own company in all the years to come. A paid agent, a liar, an unnatural vicious daughter. That's worse than the darkest cell of a dungeon.

STARBUCK (smiling). How tragically young people take life.

MADELEINE. You are always right. These are pathetic phrases to snare your sympathy. But you see us as we are, not tragic but amusing. "Do you resent the insult to your name, Mademoiselle de Tourville?" Wonderfully amusing!

STARBUCK. Why did you come to me with this confession? Why are you trying to save Nicholas from the Marquise?

MADELEINE. I never thought of trying to save Nicholas!

STARBUCK. Now you puzzle me indeed! Surely you don't simply wish to spoil your mother's good luck!

MADELEINE. No!

STARBUCK. Well then, it was your conscience. It's not so complicated after all.

MADELEINE. My conscience has been aching for many a year.

STARBUCK. Then why did you speak? Why now? Why at all? Look at me, Madeleine. (They exchange a long look again) I am inexpressibly happy.

MADELEINE. Then — may I plead for my mother again?

STARBUCK. Of course.

MADELEINE (almost stammering). Once you are safe on the mainland —

what good is a scandal to you or to Nicholas? My mother could be most useful to your side. Provided your good name is saved —

STARBUCK. What if I'm willing to sacrifice my good name?

MADELEINE (*frightened*). To expose her? To persecute her?

STARBUCK. Yes. Or to be the best man at the wedding.

MADELEINE (*dumbfounded*). What are you saying?

STARBUCK. What if my good Nicholas deserves her? What if Heaven has made this match with its fine long fingers? And what if we are four villains now instead of three?

(*MADELEINE stares*)

SCENE ELEVEN

(*Saturday, June 24. Early afternoon. The dining room at Swain's Tavern. Seated at the table: the STARBUCKS, AIMEE, WEAMISH and CUFF. AIMEE sits between the Colonel and the Captain*)

AIMEE. Someone's staring at the ceiling! (*To WEAMISH*) Yes — you, sir. We'll stand you up in the corner like a naughty boy for not doing justice to this excellent *potage*.

WEAMISH (*nervous*). I am a little preoccupied, perhaps. Several urgent cases have turned up — they fret my mind — indeed, at any moment I expect — but I deserve to be chid, for Mr. Swain keeps a pretty fair cook, old Mrs. Finney.

CUFF. Bless Mrs. Finney. This is better fare than I've tasted since I left England. Colonel, I'll trouble you for the tureen.

STARBUCK. No trouble; but hand me your plate, Captain. The Marquise will not object. A retired colonel may pour a ladle of soup into an active captain's bowl without breach of discipline.

CUFF. Ha, ha, y'are a humorous man, Colonel Starbuck. Thank you. The salt, please. A little pepper, too.

NICHOLAS. Have you asked Mr. Swain to send a bowl up to your daughter's room, Marquise? This broth will do her a world of good.

AIMEE. Thank you for your concern, Mr. Starbuck. I have given orders for a little broth, a leg of boiled chicken, and a cup of — (*she stops*)

NICHOLAS. The fatal word! Come, we're among friends. If Mr. Swain keeps a few ounces of tea in his cellar for an ailing client — I believe that even our most frenetic patriots will wink and let pass.

CUFF. Strike me dumb, but this Yankee commotion over tea is the strangest piece of foolishness that was ever heard of. For a tax of threepence on a pound of tea y'are ready to overturn the world. It makes a man mad. (*He pours an enormous quantity of salt and pepper into his soup*) Besides, don't I know, and don't the King, Lord North, Lord Germain and don't

everybody know that you smuggle in your tea from Holland anyhow? Your merchants, sir, your invoice-scribbling, bill-of-lading tradesmen can't abide to let a halfpence of profit go without raising an insurrection, bawling tyranny, ringing all the church bells, and setting the whole continent adrift. Pah! (*He pours more salt and pepper into his soup*) A sensible man must find solace in drink these days. And by God, I find I have a huge thirst in my throat. Judge: let's drink to a meeting of bullets and troublemakers.
(*WEAMISH spills his glass of wine*)
WEAMISH. Oh!
AIMEE. Oh dear!
WEAMISH. I spoiled the tablecloth!
CUFF. Fiddlesticks.
STARBUCK. Nothing of importance.
AIMEE. Is your sleeve wet, Judge?
WEAMISH. A tiny bit.
NICHOLAS. And here's another napkin. We'll spread it neatly over the scene of the crime.
WEAMISH. Thank you. . . .Forgive my clumsiness. . . .
CUFF. I'll fill your glass again.
WEAMISH (*feebly*). No . . .
(*CUFF rises to pour, then returns to his seat*)
CUFF. Here we go.
STARBUCK. Another slice of this rustic bread, Marquise?
AIMEE. Thank you. How delightful it is to dine *en petit comité* without being beset by a flock of fish-eyed servants! Shall I have the tureen taken away, Captain?
CUFF. Yes, ma'am. I'm done.
(*AIMEE rings a little bell*)
CUFF. Well, gentlemen, do I talk sense or nonsense?
STARBUCK. What about, Captain?
CUFF. That commotion over tea.
STARBUCK. Well, this is a proud nation . . .
CUFF. Nation? Y'are not a nation, says Captain Cuff, y'are a British colony, a child, a dependent, you breathe by your sovereign's grace! Too kind a rule has spoiled you, y'are lunatics of freedom, we've given you a leash five miles long and it's time we pulled it in a foot or two.
(*Enter SWAIN*)
AIMEE. Excellent *potage*, Mr. Swain. My compliments to Mrs. Finney. I'm tempted to steal her from you.
SWAIN. Thank you, Madam. I hope our joint of mutton answers your expectations.
AIMEE. I'm — Are you looking for anything, Judge?
(*WEAMISH has been anxiously peering through a window*)
WEAMISH. I? No, Marquise, not I.
(*Exit SWAIN with tureen and plates*)
AIMEE. As a Frenchwoman I am not acquainted with every particular of this

unhappy dispute between father and child — but I see so much well-being in your land that I cannot but puzzle over this rebellion.

CUFF. Spoken like a woman of sense, though French. What do you answer to that, gentlemen?

NICHOLAS. We wholeheartedly agree with Madame de Tourville. Remember that few Nantucket men have meddled in this uprising. Hence our indignation at your detaining Mr. Wallis. Let's not forget the purpose of this meeting.

CUFF. If Mr. Wallis is nothing more than a business agent, we'll return him ipso pronto to your counting house.

AIMEE. I propose that we delay this matter for a while, gentlemen. Shall we say over the fruit?

STARBUCK. As you wish, Marquise. But let me add that if Mr. Wallis is using us to screen any reprehensible action, we shall be glad to see him fettered down.

CUFF. Provided, sir, it's us that determine what is and what ain't reprehensible.

AIMEE. His Majesty is fortunate in having soldiers like yourself in his service, Captain.

CUFF. There's thousands like me.

AIMEE. We'll see you made a major or colonel presently, as there will be no lack of opportunities in America for a man of your mettle.

CUFF. There you miss the mark. I was given my captaincy twelve years ago, and I'll be pensioned the same captain I am now — unless a cannon-ball knocks my dunderhead off my shoulders before I've done my stretch.

AIMEE. This is hard to believe.

CUFF. For a lady of blood it is; not for the likes of me. It takes 2,600 pound sterling to purchase a majority in the army; I'll sooner fly to the moon than find half this money. There's many a pretty fellow giving me orders that never shot at anything but a fox or a rabbit, and never will. But they keep a dozen periwigs in their closets and smell like violets even when they belch. I have known colonels that bought a regiment they never troubled to visit, not so much as on a Sunday afternoon.

AIMEE (to STARBUCK). You were no such colonel, I hope?

STARBUCK. I hope not, Marquise.

WEAMISH. Ha! There's Jenny!

AIMEE. I beg your pardon?

WEAMISH. Outside. What can this signify? I believe she's looking for me. These urgent cases —

CUFF. What's all this?

(Enter JENNY)

JENNY (trying to sound convincing). Oh, your honor! Come quickly! We need you at home!

(She curtseys to everybody)

WEAMISH. What is it, Jenny?

AIMEE (into CUFF's ear). It's a trick — stop him!

(*The STARBUCKS are enjoying the scene*)

JENNY. It's Mr. Gardner, oh dear, oh dear —

WEAMISH (*for the gallery*). The constable.

JENNY. He says he must see your honor right away — it's about a low fellow who has been trying to break our windows —

WEAMISH. Aha! The window-breaker! Found at last! I'm coming at once! Friends —

CUFF (*rising*). No, your honor, y'are not coming at once, stab my gizzard! Our business with these gentlemen will suffer no delay. What's your name, woman?

JENNY. Jenny, sir.

CUFF. Jenny, go home, or I'll send ten raping villains to your kitchen to break your china. (*He stamps his feet*) Home! Home! Home!

(*She runs away, terrified*)

WEAMISH. But the constable!

CUFF. Can go hang himself, sir! And if he doesn't, I'll do it for him. From a Yankee Liberty Tree. (*He drinks and sits*) Sit down! Where's the mutton?

(*WEAMISH sits again*)

NICHOLAS. Thank you for staying, sir. Captain Cuff is right. We must clear up the matter of Mr. Wallis' arrest. Think of the poor man pent in a damp prison cell.

WEAMISH. But I was called! The constable!

AIMEE. I wonder where Mr. Swain is hiding with the main course.

(*She rings the bell. Enter SWAIN*)

AIMEE. The next course, Mr. Swain.

SWAIN. So sorry, Madam. Coming in a second. And done to perfection, I promise.

(*He exits*)

AIMEE. I trust you like mutton, Judge Weamish?

CUFF. A glass of water will help your voice. Here.

WEAMISH. Oh, my voice is — thank you. (*He drinks*) I — I am fond of mutton.

(*SWAIN enters and sets the meat down*)

CUFF. That's all, Mr. Swain; I'll do the carving.

SWAIN. Very good, Captain.

CUFF. Leave the door open when you go out, will you? This madeira has warmed my blood. Smuggled, I suppose.

SWAIN. Yes, sir. I mean — I'll leave the door open.

(*He leaves. The CAPTAIN carves, and places meat on everybody's plates*)

CUFF. Looks appetizing enough for a last supper.

STARBUCK. Not too generous, Captain; I've a bit of rough work ahead of me today, and I shouldn't like to get sleepy.

CUFF. Still, one never knows what the future holds; dine while you can is my motto. Your plate, Judge?

WEAMISH. Very little. I feel —

NICHOLAS. These window panes have affected you, Judge Weamish; but eat and be merry; the Captain is right.

CUFF. Thank you, Mr. Starbuck. Judge, let's hear a toast before we fall to our meat.
(*He fills all the glasses*)
WEAMISH. A toast? Now?
CUFF. Aye, a toast.
WEAMISH. This wine is not quality enough for a toast. Mr. Swain keeps a few choice bottles in his cellar — let me see to it — (*He tries to rise*)
CUFF. Rubbish. This is excellent stuff. A toast! At once!
WEAMISH (*standing up*). I propose —
CUFF. What? I can't hear you, devils in hell!
WEAMISH (*shouting*). I drink to King George —
STARBUCK (*standing up too*). And I to the United Provinces of America!
CUFF. Do you? I arrest you in the King's name!
(*AIMEE dips under the table and gives CUFF his pistol*)
STARBUCK. And we arrest you in the name of the Congress.
(*NICHOLAS and STARBUCK approach CUFF*)
CUFF. Stand back! Where's Ludley and Harrington? Stand back, traitors! Or die! (*He pulls the trigger. WEAMISH cries and faints. Nothing happens*) Who emptied my pistol?
AIMEE. I did.
(*She takes a second pistol from under the table and hands it to NICHOLAS*)
NICHOLAS. Thank you, Marquise.
(*He aims it at CUFF*)
CUFF (*stupefied*). The French jade's a rebel too!
AIMEE. Your servant, Captain Bully.
NICHOLAS. Sit down, Captain.
CUFF. Ludley! Harrington!
(*NICHOLAS pushes him down. Enter WALLIS, COFFIN and MAMACK, all armed*)
STARBUCK. Welcome, Wallis, welcome boys!
WALLIS. Well met again, Colonel, Mr. Starbuck.
COFFIN. Greetings one and all!
MAMACK. How d'ye do!
CUFF (*gaping*). Where are my men?
STARBUCK. Where are the Captain's men?
COFFIN. In the cellar, with more rope around them than a windlass.
WALLIS. And here's some left over for the Captain and the Judge. Good heavens, is the Judge dead?
NICHOLAS. No; he is momentarily absent.
(*WALLIS ties CUFF to his chair. STARBUCK closes the shutters of the room*)
CUFF. Damn your hide; I knew from the first you were no better than a Turk.
NICHOLAS. Not so much noise, Captain. This is a respectable inn.
CUFF. Enjoy yourselves, confounded rebels, but we'll see who laughs last when my men get wind of this.
STARBUCK. Did you carry out my orders, Coffin?
COFFIN. Yes, Colonel. We found the sergeant in a bathtub.
CUFF. Blast you to hell!

COFFIN. He was a little disturbed at first, but when we started to hang him naked he became friendly. He called off the villains standing guard over the jailhouse, and that's how we freed Mr. Wallis. By that time there was nearly a hundred of us besides the sergeant with a rope about his neck, seeing which, the redcoats turned their muskets over to us and wrapped their sergeant in a cloak.

NICHOLAS. Done with true British decency. But now, my friends, let us offer a round of thanks to Madame de Tourville, the future Mrs. Nicholas Starbuck, and the sole authoress of this victory.

CUFF. Good. She'll sell your scalp to the Indians. Mr. Starbuck, with her as your wife, I'm well avenged already.

MAMACK. Let him talk, Mr. Starbuck. I cry Hip, Hip, Hooray.

WEAMISH. Ooooh . . .

AIMEE. You've awakened the Judge. (*She moistens the JUDGE's face*) Come to, your honor.

COFFIN. In time to take Mr. Wallis' place in jail.

WEAMISH. Pity, my friends, intercede for me, Marquise!

CUFF. You're sending your plea to the wrong quarter, Judge. The Marquise is one of *them*.

WEAMISH. Impossible.

AIMEE. Join us, Judge. We're charming people here, and, *entre nous*, the Revolution is likely to become the fashion.

WEAMISH. Oh, Marquise, I am dizzy. How could you — ?

CUFF. She's marrying that young blackguard over there.

NICHOLAS. We could remove you at once, Captain.

CUFF. If you do, you'll be left in rotten company.

WEAMISH. The world moves too rapidly for me. Allow me to withdraw again. (*He prepares to faint*)

NICHOLAS. Steady, Judge, we need you.

WALLIS. Should I tie him up too, sir?

NICHOLAS. Tie up the Judge? Why?

STARBUCK. Why not? It will make a good impression on Governor Gage when he hears of it.

WEAMISH. Very thoughtful, Colonel. Not too tight, my friend; I shan't make any trouble.

CUFF. You didn't give much help, Judge, but I'm glad to find you're not a bloody rebel like the rest.

WEAMISH. I am a man of honor.

NICHOLAS. So much for that. Now for the toast that was so interestingly interrupted. I propose, with my uncle, the United Provinces of America, and request that Judge Weamish and Captain Cuff join their voices to ours. To America!

ALL EXCEPT CUFF AND WEAMISH. To America!

CUFF. God save the King!

COFFIN. God save the people!

CUFF. They'll need more saving than you think, you blockhead! You'll miss the King some day, all you raggle-taggle levellers — when high and low are topsy-turvy — when your drunken cobblers write your laws — and when y'are ruled by ambitious grocers. God save the King! I'm dumb from now on.

NICHOLAS. That will be appreciated by all. Carry him into the cellar, Mamack, let him confer below with his two henchmen.

COFFIN. I'll help.

CUFF. Remove me from this kennel, dogs. I'm grateful to you.

(*They carry CUFF out in his chair, and later return*)

STARBUCK (*pulling a couple of documents out of his pocket*). My dear Judge, I apologize for the start we gave you. Be assured, however, that our personal esteem for you remains unaltered.

WEAMISH. Likewise, Colonel Starbuck. These are political differences —

STARBUCK. It would give us a world of pleasure if we could reconcile them.

WEAMISH. Well, I'm human. Ah, Marquise, was it all deceit? Were you never in Governor Gage's service as you led me to believe?

NICHOLAS. What does he mean, Madame?

AIMEE. Bah! I told the Judge a fib in order the better to arrange this dinner. Forgive me, sir; but war is hard on a woman's delicacy.

WEAMISH. Alas. But were you never —

AIMEE. Tut, tut. What are these papers, Colonel Starbuck?

WEAMISH. Yes, what are they, my dear Colonel?

STARBUCK. Your resignation from the bench, Mr. Weamish.

WEAMISH. My resignation from the bench? This is a blow. Hm. Why not talk it over in my study, Colonel? Here is something else.

STARBUCK. Yes. An order for the arrests of Dr. Tupper, Mr. Applegate —

WEAMISH. Mr. Applegate! But he's a guest in Nantucket!

NICHOLAS. Damn your mincing and wincing, Weamish! Applegate is a Tory; he'll be arrested or I'll become King George's bootblack.

(*He pokes WEAMISH's nose with the barrel of his pistol*)

WEAMISH. You know best, Mr. Starbuck. (*NICHOLAS removes the pistol*) Thank you. And who else? Not Mr. Folger! Not Mr. Mayhew! Not Mr. Rotch!

STARBUCK. Only for a few weeks, Judge.

WEAMISH. I thought I was no longer on the bench.

STARBUCK. You will first sign this warrant — we'll free your writing hand, don't be anxious on that account — and then your resignation. Our Committee of Safety —

WEAMISH. Have we a Committee of Safety? In Nantucket?

STARBUCK. We have.

WEAMISH. Bless my soul!

STARBUCK. The Committee desires that royal appointments like your own be surrendered forthwith and reconfirmed by ourselves. Our selectmen and assessors, the town clerk and the treasurer have all sworn allegiance to the principles of liberty. If you decide to emulate them, I'll venture the guess that no one will insist upon a new Justice of the Peace.

WEAMISH. I must think it over. Too many events have whirled about my head. I must await my mother's return.

STARBUCK (*loosening the ropes*). At your leisure. Pray place your name here.

WEAMISH. Under duress?

WALLIS. I think we should hang him, sir.

COFFIN. The sign at the door will hold him snugly. I know Mr. Swain won't mind hardly at all.

NICHOLAS. I'm with you. Our Tories need an example; one Justice in a noose will knock sense into five hundred heads.

AIMEE. May I intercede for him, my love? He has entertained me ever so courteously.

NICHOLAS. No, angel; not this time; forgive me; but the enemies of our nation must be exterminated. Take him away, lads.

WEAMISH. No!

MAMACK. Sorry, Judge.

WEAMISH. Wait! This is a jest, I know! (*The others make a move*) But I'll sign. I'm fond of a little foolery myself. There.

STARBUCK. Thank you, Mr. Weamish. Here's a glass of madeira.

WEAMISH. It *will* soothe my nerves a little.

AIMEE. Poor dear.

STARBUCK. Mamack, run to Constable Gardner with this document and ask him to enforce it at once.

MAMACK. Yes, sir.

(*He leaves. Starbuck sets WEAMISH free*)

STARBUCK. Farewell, Mr. Weamish. We shall not meet again for many a stormy day. Will you give me your hand? (*They shake hands*) Reconsider, and join our cause. We are not saints. God knows I have told my share of lies and gone by crooked ways. But all in all, Tom, I am your elder — and a wiser head than you: we are the better men, believe me, and the future is with us.

WEAMISH. I promise to think it over.

NICHOLAS. Bring Mrs. Weamish round as well.

AIMEE. As for myself, I'll not forget your kind welcome, Judge. I shall always keep a set of rooms ready for you — here in America, or at my chateau in Gascony.

WEAMISH. Will you have me, Marquise?

AIMEE. As long as I live.

(*She gives him her hand; he kisses it*)

WEAMISH. Blood always tells.

(*He leaves*)

AIMEE. Still, one cannot deny him the title of gentleman, my dear.

NICHOLAS. Nor that of conclusive fool, my love.

STARBUCK. Wallis, you shall see that Cuff and his troopers are safely transferred to the mainland and delivered to the Congress. The ladies, young Nick and myself will cross on the *Enterprise* as arranged beforehand, since there will be messages awaiting me on board. Is it set for tonight, Mr. Coffin?

COFFIN. Everything is ready.

STARBUCK. Gentlemen, thank you again. Each man to his post.

(*They shake hands; farewells ad libitum, WALLIS and COFFIN leave*)

NICHOLAS. Well, uncle, are you pleased?

STARBUCK. I am. My dear lady, I ought now to display a power of eloquence to thank you, but I believe my nephew is willing to express our obligation for both of us.

AIMEE. I want no thanks. I am now in your family, Colonel, for better or for worse, and owe you the poor talents and resources that I command. Instead of idle ceremony, let us look after my daughter; we must try to dissuade her from her gloomy purpose to return to a land she has never known. Will you assist me, husband? And you, dear uncle?

STARBUCK. Gladly.

NICHOLAS. After you, Marquise.

AIMEE. Is not this the Captain's bumper? It never did reach his lips! (*She raises the glass*) I'll see you all fried in whale oil, says Captain Cuff!

(*Laughter*)

SCENE TWELVE

(Saturday, June 24. Before dark. At the seaside as in Scene Seven. COFFIN is sitting by the fishing-stage, whittling, and singing)

COFFIN.   You must make me a fine Holland shirt,
                           Blow, blow, blow, ye winds, blow
                           And not have in it a stitch of needlework,
                           Blow, ye winds that arise, blow, blow.

                           You must wash it in yonder spring,
                           Blow, blow, blow, ye winds, blow,
                           Where there's never a drop of water in,
                           Blow, ye winds that arise, blow, blow.

(Enter STARBUCK and NICHOLAS carrying small travel cases)
COFFIN. Greetings.
(They shake hands)
STARBUCK. Ready for us, Obed?
COFFIN. All ready. And the ladies?
STARBUCK. Following us with baggage. *(Looking toward the sea)* She's waiting for us, is she?
COFFIN. She dropped anchor about an hour ago and signalled.
STARBUCK. Well, daylight is waning, so let's set off as soon as possible.
COFFIN. I thought Mamack would be here with you.
NICHOLAS. No, we sent him back with the horses. I think I hear the chaise with our women.
(He exits)
COFFIN. We're mighty proud of you, General Starbuck. We'll guard your property here like what's his name, the dog in Hades. When you come back, you'll find every speck of it the same as you left it, or never trust me again.
STARBUCK. When I come back. Who knows? I fear that streams of blood will be shed before heaven decides who will stand and who must fall.

COFFIN. I hear there's talk of conciliation yet. Perhaps you'll be back sooner than we all expect.

STARBUCK. I want to believe it. And yet — these men who mean to rule us by the birch as if we were children — they are not evil men — but they are blind — and that's where my heart misgives — for it's often easier to deal with an informed villain than with a well-intentioned dunce.

COFFIN. We'll pray for the best.

STARBUCK. And work for it, and fight for it.

COFFIN. Here they come.

(Enter AIMEE, MADELEINE and NICHOLAS)

STARBUCK. Welcome, welcome!

MADELEINE. Thank you.

AIMEE. How pleasant to see this spot again! Eh, you rascal?

NICHOLAS (kissing her fingers). Obed, you must lend me a hand.

COFFIN. Yes, sir.

(They leave)

AIMEE. What, General Starbuck, no farewell committee? No band of musicians? No flowers?

STARBUCK. No, no, nothing of the sort. We leave quietly. There's too much bad blood in Nantucket as it is. My heart aches when I think I am in part guilty of it.

AIMEE. You are a lamb, General, believe me; I know mankind, if anyone does, and I say to you, you are a holy lamb.

MADELEINE. Mother!

AIMEE. My cousin on my mother's side, the Chevalier de Cassefer, once tore a Prussian's left arm from the shoulder with his bare two hands.

STARBUCK. I shall try to deal more humanely with our enemy — who, when all is said and done, remains our brother.

AIMEE. The Chevalier behaved worse to his brother.

MADELEINE. Mother, mother, no more family stories, I beg you.

AIMEE. The poor girl is sensitive for our reputation. Ah, here come our helpers. Gently, my friends, there's porcelain in my trunk.

(NICHOLAS and COFFIN are carrying a huge trunk)

COFFIN. Let's take it directly to the boat, Mr. Starbuck.

NICHOLAS. Let's indeed.

AIMEE. That's a bit harder than rescuing a man from the sea, I'll wager.

NICHOLAS. It is, and I hope for a sweeter reward accordingly.

AIMEE. Ogre!

(NICHOLAS and COFFIN pass off the stage)

AIMEE. Shall we have a tranquil passage, Elias? I may call you Elias, I hope.

STARBUCK. Of course. I believe we shall. And a brief one, too.

AIMEE. You will call me Aimée, will you not?

STARBUCK. With pleasure.

(Reenter NICHOLAS and COFFIN)

NICHOLAS. Now for Madeleine's.

(They leave again)

STARBUCK. Did you find time to take leave of the Judge, my dear Aimée?

AIMEE. Yes, we both went to pay our respects. But we found him very low, lying on a sofa, complaining of dizzy spells, and inhaling salts.

STARBUCK. Poor fellow.

(*Reenter NICHOLAS and COFFIN, carrying a very small portmanteau — MADELEINE's*)

COFFIN. I'll take it to the boat myself, Mr. Starbuck.

NICHOLAS. How is it that our Madeleine is carrying so much less than you, angel?

AIMEE. Immaturity, dear. Idealism travels light; but when ideals wear thin, property becomes a comfort.

NICHOLAS. And what am I — your ideal or your property?

AIMEE. Come here, you puppy. You are — my ideal property.

(*Reenter COFFIN*)

COFFIN. I'm afraid we'll have to make two trips. My boat cannot hold five and a trunk.

NICHOLAS. No matter. Uncle, you go first with Madeleine. We'll follow.

STARBUCK. No; I'll follow *you*. Let me linger here another hour and gently loosen my last roots. Madeleine will keep me company.

NICHOLAS. As you wish. Ready, angel?

AIMEE. Ready. (*She kisses MADELEINE*) I'll see you presently, dearest. If the water is choppy, close your eyes and think of babies in cradles.

MADELEINE. Yes, Mother.

NICHOLAS. Stop!

AIMEE. What is it?

(*NICHOLAS sweeps her up into his arms*)

AIMEE. Rape!

NICHOLAS. My prize! My glorious prize!

(*He carries her off*)

STARBUCK (*after him*). Don't stumble, Nicholas, don't drop your prize!

(*STARBUCK and MADELEINE are left alone. STARBUCK sits down by the fishing-stage, closes his eyes, and breathes deeply. MADELEINE begins to move quietly away. STARBUCK opens his eyes*)

STARBUCK. Where are you going, Madeleine?

MADELEINE. Only a little farther off.

STARBUCK. Why?

MADELEINE. I — I wanted to leave you to yourself.

STARBUCK. To punish me for my wickedness?

MADELEINE. What wickedness??

STARBUCK. With respect to your mother, perhaps.

MADELEINE. Oh yes! I accuse you of being too unfailingly kind; of pretending too beautifully that you know nothing.

STARBUCK. Are you sure it's the beauty of it which struck you?

MADELEINE. I don't understand.

STARBUCK. I almost thought a while ago that my light-heartedness — why, that it very nearly distressed you.

MADELEINE. It made me feel even more ashamed.

STARBUCK. But something else besides. Perhaps, in your imagination of me, you wanted to see me, oh, struggle at least to suppress a touch of censoriousness.

MADELEINE (*smiling*). Where can I hide from you?

STARBUCK. But I never could take a high moral tone, Madeleine. You must bear with me. I can't fly into a passion over every human delinquency. I keep my fund of rage in reserve for great occasions.

MADELEINE. I wish I could learn from you!

STARBUCK. Do you really?

MADELEINE. Of course. Can you doubt it?

STARBUCK. Beware! I am an old man, fifty-four years old. This means that I have amassed a huge store of useful knowledge. Even Madame Pichot's trunk couldn't hold it all. It would take me years to unload it, sort it out, and bequeath it to you.

MADELEINE. If only it could be done in an hour, before the boat returns. I shall sorely need it.

STARBUCK. Impossible. A lifetime is necessary. (*She turns her head away*) What is it, Madeleine?

MADELEINE. Nothing. You wanted to say farewell to your island, Colonel. General.

STARBUCK. What will you do with your lifetime instead?

MADELEINE. Is this not a cruel question?

STARBUCK. Presently I will give you a chance to be cruel with me in return.

MADELEINE. I never seem to understand you!

STARBUCK. My wisdom I can impart to you in much less than an hour, Madeleine. It is my love it would take me a lifetime to unfold. (*Silence*) You see, now you can be cruel with me in a large way.

MADELEINE (*low*). My mother is a swindler, a spy, a nobody, a libertine. I am her bastard, a pauper, a nobody, and a sparkless one besides. How would you deal with me if I had not almost a pretty face?

STARBUCK. I would love, admire, and defend you, above all against yourself. Your beauty, I confess, has shamefully unhinged me, to the point of asking you to be my wife as if I were a catch for a girl of twenty. But I fancy that your good sense will keep you at a safe distance from me.

MADELEINE. Because I would not disgrace you.

STARBUCK. Madeleine is always gentle.

MADELEINE. Because I would not disgrace you, Elias.

STARBUCK. Look at these miserable wrinkles. Think of my grey hair. Or no hair at all!

MADELEINE (*weeping*). Don't abandon me . . .

STARBUCK. Could you bear me as a husband?

(*She flings herself into his arms*)

MADELEINE. Care for me! I'll please you, you'll see! I shall try so bravely that you'll be proud of your foundling!

STARBUCK. Such wild words! I'll care for you like an old hound standing guard over a treasure. But why take me as a husband? Your friend Starbuck will do it as well, I swear, and he'll slink off the moment you appoint a more tasteful husband.

MADELEINE (*holding him*). Are you turning me away already? So soon?

STARBUCK. Mine then. Mine to the end of my blessed time.

MADELEINE. Yours for as long as you will keep me.

(*They kiss*)

MADELEINE (*touching his cheeks, eyes, and forehead with her fingers*). So fine, so strong, so merry, so wise . . .

STARBUCK. Wise indeed, to have bewitched you into my arms and condemned you —

MADELEINE. To be a lifelong burden to you!

STARBUCK. Yes, the way a flower burdens the earth.

MADELEINE. Hold me. Your flower is shivering.

STARBUCK. The sun is setting and the wind is beginning to blow. Is this better?

MADELEINE. Much better.

(*Silence*)

STARBUCK. Look!

MADELEINE. Must I?

STARBUCK. Look who reappeared beyond that spit of land. To remind us that we are not in heaven, I suppose! But what is Nicholas doing? I believe he is singing, on my word!

MADELEINE. Mother is pointing at us. .

STARBUCK. They're waving! (*Both wave back*) Romantic couple!

MADELEINE. Oh, I'm so afraid for them.

STARBUCK. Why, Madeleine?

MADELEINE. I don't know . . . What will happen when Nicholas discovers that he married Madame Pichot? For surely he *will* discover it sooner or later.

STARBUCK. Why, he'll fume for a while, but his interest will be the same as hers: to bury the truth.

MADELEINE. You don't imagine that he'll turn her out into the street?

STARBUCK. Never!

MADELEINE. My mother was less confident. She took precautions. (*She produces a letter and gives it to STARBUCK*)

STARBUCK. What's this? A letter to Nicholas? From Ezekiel Davis! How did this come into your hands?

MADELEINE. Mother filched it from Nick's case this afternoon, and gave it to me for safekeeping. I am betraying her again.

STARBUCK (*reading*). "Our Mrs. Applegate grows desperate; she has indeed every power to sell the estate. Give us some useful intelligence, true or false, concerning Mr. Applegate, and our Sons of Liberty shall rattle Mrs. A., I assure you, till she will sell to yours truly, and gratefully too, for ten shillings in the pound." (*With deep bitterness*) Ten shillings in the pound is handsome! Good work, nephew. No wonder you're singing. (*His head sinks*)

MADELEINE (*frightened*). What have I done? I'm a fool!

STARBUCK. No, no; you did well; I must try to save this woman . . .

MADELEINE. I've given you pain — already!

STARBUCK (*vehemently*). Salutary pain. It's about time the truth took me by the throat. I have been too neighborly with the beast. Tomorrow on the Sabbath, while you and I kneel in thanksgiving, young Nick — but what am I saying? Every Tom, Nick and Harry will be busy buying cheap and selling dear, abusing the ignorant, hoarding scarce goods, making hyena profits from our war, and sucking the sap out of the land. There's the truth at last. But now what? Where shall I find the strength?

MADELEINE. How I want to comfort you . . .

STARBUCK. Should we even begin?

MADELEINE. Tomorrow we shall be on the mainland.

(*STARBUCK walks to the water's edge and stares outward*)

STARBUCK. Should we even begin?

(*MADELEINE joins him, takes his hand, and kisses it*)

MADELEINE. Not, at any rate, with our eyes closed.

(*Long silence*)

STARBUCK. With our eyes open then. So be it.

THE END